ifast
BOOK TWO

THE REPAIRER OF THE BREACH

CEPHAS KAFUI

The Repairer of the Breach

CEPHAS KAFUI

ifast – The Repairer of the Breach

Copyright © 2020 by Cephas Agbesi
ifast – Book Two: The Repairer of the Breach by Cephas Kafui

Copyright book cover artwork by Cephas Agbesi

Published by Prayer Cell Publications

Printed in the United States of America
First Edition

ISBN 978-1-7346144-0-4

All rights reserved solely by the author. No part of this publication may be reproduced, stored in a retrieval system, or transmitted in any form or by any means – for example, electronic photocopy, recording – without the prior written permission of the author. The only exception is brief quotations in printed reviews.

For information about permission to reproduce selections from this book, write to permissions@prayercell.com

Unless otherwise indicated, Bible quotations are taken from King James Version of the Holy Bible.

Cover design by Image and Like Studio
www.imlkstudio.com

Edited by Honorable Vivienne E. Gordon-Uruakpa

Credit

This work will not have been completed without the help of several individuals, of whom the length of space will not permit me to mention names. I am duly grateful for the support and love of the Honeywell Worship Center members in New York, my organic wife Alrecia and to our three children; the blessings of my parents Martin and Victoria and my dear siblings. I acknowledge the spiritual guidance of Apostle Dr. Eric Achaab, of whom I have benefited greatly. Cheers to Dr. Juliet Appiah (MD), who has been a wonderful resource to my ministry. I am indebted to Daniel Essuah of Image and Likeness Studio for all artworks and designs. Finally, I am beholden to Honorable Vivienne E. Gordon-Uruakpa for taking time to proofread yet another book for me.

CONTENT

PREFACE 1

THE LAW OF FASTING 1

UNDERSTANDING THE ANCIENT MYSTERY OF FASTING 5

FASTING IN ISLAM 6
FASTING IN JUDAISM 7
FASTING IN BUDDHISM 9
FASTING IN HINDUISM 12
AN APPEAL TO THE CHRISTIAN 14

THEIR GOD IS THEIR STOMACH 16

REPAIRER OF THE BREACH 27

HOW TO BEGIN 34

TYPES OF FASTING 34
FIFTEEN WAYS TO FAST 36
A MESSAGE TO FAMILIES ABOUT PRAYER AND FASTING TOGETHER 37
FORMAT: THE 30-DAY FASTING GUIDE 38
BREAKING THE FAST 40
CHOICE OF FOOD: THE DANIEL FAST PRINCIPLE 40
FOODS TO AVOID ON THE FAST 42
SUGGESTED DAILY GUIDE FOR JUICE FAST 43
HOW TO FINISH YOUR FAST IN A HEALTHY WAY 44
PRE-FAST CAUTION 45
DURING THE FAST 45
SYMPTOMS DURING A PROLONGED FAST: 47

DAY 1	51
HYPOCRISY	51
LOG-ON: DAY 1 – MORNING PRAYERS	52
DAY 1	54
HYPOCRISY	54
LOG-OFF: DAY 1 - EVENING PRAYERS	60
DAY 2	62
THE FALSE PURSUIT OF GOD	62
LOG-ON: DAY 2 – MORNING PRAYERS	63
DAY 2	65
THE FALSE PURSUIT OF GOD	65
LOG-OFF: DAY 2 - EVENING PRAYERS	70
DAY 3	72
THE FASTING GOD DESPISES	72
LOG-ON: DAY 3 – MORNING PRAYERS	73
DAY 3	75
THE FASTING GOD DESPISES	75

LOG-OFF: DAY 3 – EVENING PRAYERS	79
DAY 4	80
FASTING WITHOUT GOD	80
LOG-ON: DAY 4 – MORNING PRAYERS	81
DAY 4	84
THE FAST WITHOUT GOD	84
LOG-OFF: DAY 4 – EVENING PRAYERS	88
DAY 5	90
THE TONGUE IN FASTING	90
LOG-ON: DAY 5 – MORNING PRAYERS	91
DAY 5	93
THE TONGUE IN FASTING	93
LOG-ON: DAY 5 – EVENING PRAYERS	97
DAY 6	98
THE REJECTED FAST	98
LOG-ON: DAY 6 – MORNING PRAYERS	99
DAY 6	102

THE REJECTED FAST 102

LOG-OFF: DAY 6 – EVENING PRAYERS 106

DAY 7 107

BREAKING THE CHAINS OF WICKEDNESS 107

LOG-ON: DAY 7 – MORNING PRAYERS 108

DAY 7 110

BREAKING THE CHAINS OF WICKEDNESS 110

LOG-OFF: DAY 7 – EVENING PRAYERS 114

DAY 8 115

THE HEAVY BURDENS 115

LOG-ON: DAY 8 – MORNING PRAYERS 116

DAY 8 118

THE HEAVY BURDENS 118

LOG-OFF: DAY 8 – EVENING PRAYERS 122

DAY 9 124

FREEDOM FROM OPPRESSION 124

LOG-ON: DAY 9 – MORNING PRAYERS 125

DAY 9	127
FREEDOM FROM OPPRESSION	127
LOG-OFF: DAY 9 – EVENING PRAYERS	142
DAY 10	143
THE YOKE BREAKER	143
LOG-ON: DAY 10 – MORNING PRAYERS	144
DAY 10	145
THE YOKE BREAKER	145
LOG-OFF: DAY 10 – EVENING PRAYERS	150
DAY 11	151
INCONVENIENT GIVING	151
LOG-ON: DAY 11 – MORNING PRAYERS	152
DAY 11	154
INCONVENIENT GIVING	154
LOG-OFF: DAY 11 – EVENING PRAYERS	158
DAY 12	159
SACRIFICIAL GIVING	159

LOG-ON: DAY 12 – MORNING PRAYERS	160
DAY 12	163
SACRIFICIAL GIVING	163
LOG-OFF: DAY 12 – EVENING PRAYERS	167
DAY 13	169
THE LIGHT OF THE WORLD	169
LOG-ON: DAY 13 – MORNING PRAYERS	170
DAY 13	173
THE LIGHT OF THE WORLD	173
LOG-OFF: DAY 13 - EVENING PRAYERS	176
DAY 14	177
FAST HEALING	177
LOG-ON: DAY 14 – MORNING PRAYERS	178
DAY 14	180
FAST HEALING	180
LOG-OFF: DAY 14 – EVENING PRAYERS	183
DAY 15	184

THE GIFT OF RIGHTEOUSNESS 184

LOG-ON: DAY 15 – MORNING PRAYERS 185

DAY 15 187

THE GIFT OF RIGHTEOUSNESS 187

LOG-OFF: DAY 15 – EVENING PRAYERS 191

DAY 16 192

GOD'S GOT YOUR BACK 192

LOG-OFF: DAY 16 – MORNING PRAYERS 193

DAY 16 195

GOD'S GOT YOUR BACK 195

WHEN DO YOU NEED A "REAR GUARD"? 195
LOG-OFF: DAY 16 – EVENING PRAYERS 200

DAY 17 201

POWER THROUGH FASTING 201

LOG-ON: DAY 17 – MORNING PRAYERS 202

DAY 17 204

POWER THROUGH DESTINY 204

LOG-OFF: EVENING PRAYERS	209
DAY 18	211
THE HEART OF THE FAST	211
LOG-ON: DAY 18 – MORNING PRAYERS	212
DAY 18	214
TH HEART OF THE FAST	214
LOG-OFF: DAY 18 - EVENING PRAYER	216
DAY 19	218
THE BREAKING POINT	218
LOG-ON: DAY 19 – MORNING PRAYERS	219
DAY 19	221
THE BREAKING POINT	221
LOG-OFF: DAY 19 – EVENING PRAYERS	224
DAY 20	226
THE LIGHT SHINES IN DARKNESS	226
LOG-ON: DAY 20 – MORNING PRAYER	227
DAY 20	229

THE LIGHT SHINES IN DARKNESS 229

LOG-OFF: Day 20 – Evening Prayer 232

DAY 21 234

KINGDOM TRANSFORMERS 234

LOG-ON: DAY 21 – Morning Prayers 235

DAY 21 237

KINGDOM TRANSFORMERS 237

LOG-OFF: Day 21 – Evening Prayers 240

DAY 22 242

THE REPAIRER OF THE BREACH 242

LOG-ON: DAY 22 – Morning Prayers 243

DAY 22 245

REPAIRER OF THE BREACH PART 1 245

LOG-OFF: DAY 22 – Evening Prayers 247

DAY 23 248

REPAIRER OF THE BREACH PART 2 248

LOG-ON: DAY 23 – Morning Prayers 249

DAY 23 251

REPAIRER OF THE BREACH PART 2 251

LOG-OFF: DAY 23 – EVENING PRAYERS 253

DAY 24 255

REPAIRER OF THE BREACH PART 3 255

LOG-ON: DAY 24 – MORNING PRAYERS 256

DAY 24 258

REPAIRER OF THE BREACH PART 3 258

LOG-OFF: DAY 24 – EVENING PRAYERS 261

DAY 25 263

THE HOLY DAY 263

LOG-ON: DAY 25 – MORNING PRAYERS 264

DAY 25 266

THE HOLY DAY 266

LOG-OFF: DAY 25 – EVENING PRAYERS 269

DAY 26 270

REMOVING SPIRITUAL BREACHES 270

LOG-ON: DAY 26 – MORNING PRAYERS 271

DAY 26 272

REMOVING SPIRITUAL BREACHES 272

LOG-OFF: DAY 26 – EVENING PRAYERS 274

DAY 27 275

HOW TO DETECT PERSONAL BREACHES 275

LOG-ON: DAY 27 – MORNING PRAYERS 276

DAY 27 278

HOW TO DETECT PERSONAL BREACHES 278

LOG-OFF: DAY 27 – EVENING PRAYERS 281

DAY 28 282

HOW TO DETECT PERSONAL BREACHES II 282

LOG-ON: DAY 28 – MORNING PRAYERS 283

DAY 28 285

HOW TO DETECT PERSONAL BREACHES II 285

LOG-OFF: DAY 28 – EVENING PRAYERS 289

DAY 29 291

THE MINISTRY OF RESTORATION 291

LOG-ON: DAY 29 – MORNING PRAYERS 292

DAY 29 294

THE MINISTRY OF RESTORATION 294

LOG OFF: DAY 29 – EVENING PRAYERS 296

DAY 30 299

THE MASTER REPAIRER 299

LOG-ON: DAY 30 – MORNING PRAYERS 300

DAY 30 302

THE MASTER REPAIRER 302

LOG OFF: DAY 30 – EVENING PRAYERS 306

POSTFACE 309

BREAKING THE FAST 309

A WORD OF CAUTION 310
TESTIMONY 311

Preface
The Law of Fasting

FASTING IS THE LAW of abstinence from food for the development of spiritual strength. It is an expression of humility, sacrifice and dependence on God. Fasting in the Bible is abstinence from food, not abstention from activities such as social media, internet, television or junk foods. Biblical fasting is the absolute self-denial of all food, or the partial abstention from specific foods for spiritual emphasis for a period of time.

In fact, the Hebrew word "tsowm (twoom), which is translated "fast" or "fasting" means "to cover the mouth." Likewise, the Greek word "nesteuo (nace-tyoo) which is in our translation "fast," means "to abstain food." Therefore, fasting in the Bible was done by abstaining from food, though it mostly requires refraining from activities so one can focus on fellowship with Yahweh.

Fasting is more about replacing than it is about abstaining. Fasting is replacing the daily intakes of food, entertainment, and human contact with focused times of prayer, feeding on large amounts of the Word of God and spiritual listening. One of the great benefits of spiritual fasting is a heightened awareness of God's presence and power in our lives. It is not that God has moved, but that we have. Fasting has a great way of moving us toward a deeper spiritual dependency and away from willful self-dependency.

The practice of fasting is not new to religion. In fact, all religions place a strong emphasis on fasting as a principle for spiritual strength, enlightenment into supernatural mysteries, and an extension of mortality to commune with immortality. In fasting, the mortal man is able to communicate in deeper intimacy with the immortal supernatural creatures.

As believers, we must not fast because it is a law in the Old Testament of the Bible. We must understand that Biblical fasting was not instituted at the establishment of the Day of Atonement for Israel. The fast as we know it in the Scriptures, predates the Mosaic Laws. It is an ancient invention, that can be traced back to the Paradise of Eden. It was the first commandment Adam received from Yahweh: *"but of the tree of the knowledge of good and evil you shall not eat..."* (Genesis 2:17). With the crescendo of that phrase, "you shall not eat" the first law of humankind is established.

There is no commandment in all of scripture given to humankind, that is as ancient as the Law of the Fast. Our first parents, Adam and Eve were commanded to fast and abstain from the Tree of the Knowledge of Good and Evil. Yahweh did not suggest to them, but He commanded of them not to eat. Though the current Christian theology is well-defined on the subject of fasting and submits that fasting is not a Christian requirement, I believe on the basis of scriptures that Yahweh demands that we fast of a necessity from certain things in our lives. The test of Adam and Eve is a test that we will all face in our lives. We cannot grow in spiritual strength until we practice the Law of Fasting. Adam and Eve lost paradise the day they broke this code. Their intimate relationship with Yahweh was dependent on their capacity to abstain from eating of that tree. Had our first parents denied themselves of eating of this tree, we would not be here today fasting. Since they were unsuccessful, we must now do what they could not, which is to fast.

The relationship between Adam and Eve and God was based on their self-denial. If they could continue fasting every day from that tree, they would continue to be in direct and consistent fellowship with Yahweh. They would enjoy Yahweh's presence, as long as they maintained their abstinence. Angels entertained and visited them daily because they were in fasting often. This I believe is the mystery behind Apostle Paul's decision to remain in *"fasting often"* (2 Corinthians 11:27). We are invited into immortal companionship with Yahweh through the Law of Fasting; if we can practice self-denial, then we can have time and space to receive Him.

There is no Paradise, no Eden without Fasting. This Paradise given to our first parents was architecturally built by the hands and wisdom of God. It was divine; it was glorious; it was majestic without an iota of flaw found in it; because the hand of Yahweh had made it. Nevertheless, it was to be maintained by fasting: *"you shall not eat"* says Yahweh. This they failed tragically.

Do you want an Eden in your life? Do you desire the Paradise of Yahweh? Have you ever imagined what Eden looked like? What if I told you it is possible to experience this Paradise, the place where Yahweh and His angels dwell? The mystery is that they lost Paradise because they did not fast, but we will gain it through fasting. We must not make the mistake of Adam and his wife Eve who listened to the counsel of the ancient serpent (the devil). He will tempt us even as he did Jesus. He will provoke us to compromise our destiny by eating when God has said, *"you shall not eat."* The devil will cause us to break our fasting earlier than we design, and in effect collapse our relationship with Yahweh. May we not fall to the snare of this cunning demon. May we obey the voice that is still whispering to us, *"you can have everything in this Paradise, if you do not eat of this one tree in the midst of it."* Can we refrain from one meal or two, or perhaps three, that we may gain the greater blessings of Yahweh?

Why will you not fast? The blessing is greater than the sacrifice: And the Lord God commanded the man, saying, *"Of every tree of the garden you may freely eat; but of the tree of the knowledge of good and evil you shall not eat, for in the day that you eat of it you shall surely die."* – Genesis 2:16-17

The blessing is through fasting, the intimacy is by fasting, the presence is by fasting, and divine prosperity is by fasting. Nonetheless, if we will not fast, we will end up like our first parents, Adam and Eve. We will lose the higher blessings. In fact, those who do not fast are on the road to perdition. They are cast out of the presence of God; they are thrown out of Paradise.

In brief, that great prince of the Methodist foundation, John Wesley puts it to us in this manner: "The man who never fasts is no more on the way to heaven than the man who never prays". (John Wesley, *Causes of Inefficacy of Christianity*).

This great founder of the Methodist Church, made it a rule not to ordain anyone into ministry unless they committed to fast twice a week. There is a demand for fasting in the pulpit and pews today; a return to Paradise. Now then, may this book ignite this fire of the Law of Fasting in you.

1

Understanding the Ancient Mystery of Fasting

"Then the disciples of John came to Him, saying, "Why do we and the Pharisees fast often, but Your disciples do not fast?"
– Matthew 9:14

HERE LIES A SHAMEFUL INDICTMENT of the modern church of Jesus: *"Your disciples do not fast."*

The disciples of John made a direct and frontal attack upon the LORD Jesus in the days of His ministry. They said unto Him: *"Why do we fast often…but your disciples don't?"*

This pivotal question ought to concern every believer of the Church today. We can all agree on the validity of this question by the disciples of John. It seems all other religions have placed a greater emphasis on fasting, than we the Christians.

Fasting In Islam

The Muslim, a believer of Islam, prays five times a day, and fasts for thirty days every year during the period of Ramadan. The fasting season of Ramadan is a time to develop the Muslim's moral character and focus on the positive grace given by Allah (the god of Islam). This annual fast of the Ramadan season is one of the Five Pillars of Islam.

The Muslim has placed a high value on the spiritual exercise of fasting above all else. A single drop of water on the Muslim's lips during the fast is a defilement and a condemnation of the entire fast. In some countries, it's a crime not to fast. For example, during the period of Ramadan, an adult seen eating in public in Saudi Arabia or the United Arab Emirates can be fined or jailed. Aside from legal implications, not fasting is a major sin, worse than adultery or drunkenness in Islam.

What's more, the standard in Islam is so high that during Ramadan, the Muslim is not allowed to have sex (even in a legal marriage), should not swear, smoke, be entangled in arguments or gossips. The fasting period in Islam is sacred, and devoid of sin in the life of the Muslim.

Can we then pause to ask the question again, *"why do you, the disciples of Jesus not fast?"* Child of God, do you fast? When you do fast, do you place such high value and seriousness on your fast as the Muslims do? Do you completely abstain from sin when you fast?

Why do other religions fast, and the disciples of Jesus eat and drink?

Fasting In Judaism

In Judaism, the professing Jew is obligated to fast on the Day of Atonement or what is rightly called, Yom Kippur. They believe this to be the period to examine and repent from their sins. It is required of all faithful Jews to consecrate this period to confessing their sins, and getting right with God. This is without comparison, the holiest and most important day of the Jewish religion. During the fast, they are required to seek after people they have offended, or those who have offended them, and make amends. They are not allowed to go through the fasting period with unforgiveness in their hearts toward anyone, irrespective of the sins committed against them.

The fast for the Jew, is a holy day spent exclusively at the synagogue (the Jewish temple), praying, worshiping and repenting of all sins. The Torah reads, *"The tenth day of this seventh month is the Day of Atonement. You are to hold a sacred assembly and practice self-denial; you are to present a fire offering to the LORD"* (Leviticus 23:27). Fasting in Judaism is one of self-denial. It's a day of intense self-searching, self-assessment, and fervent communication with the LORD God.

It is imperative to note that a Jew will not repent without fasting. One Jewish educator, Aliza Bulow remarked that, "...repenting without fasting is not enough." For the Jew, the gravity of sin requires fasting to completely purge one's self from inner weaknesses and absolute alienation of one's immoralities. Hence, they believe fasting to be the affliction of the soul, self-awakening, and unity with God's due order.

Like the Muslims, the Jews forbid all manner of work and activities on the days of fasting, for the soul is to be afflicted:

> *This is to be a lasting ordinance for you: On the tenth day of the seventh month you must deny yourselves and not do any work—whether native-born or a foreigner residing among you— because on this day atonement will be made for you, to cleanse you. Then, before the Lord, you will be clean from all your sins. It is a day of sabbath rest, and you must deny yourselves; it is a lasting ordinance.– Leviticus 16:29-31*

The truth is that we in the church of Jesus today do not place such importance on our fasting days. Fasting as it is practiced in the Bible is not as we do today. We have completely deviated from God's divine mandate of the fast, and what Prophet Isaiah calls, "the chosen Fast". (Isaiah 58:6).

In fact, the Jewish fasting day of Yom Kippur was so sacred that none was exempted from the practice. Once again, just as the Muslims, it was a capital crime for any professing Jew to refuse to fast:

> *"And ye shall do no work in that same day: for it is a day of atonement, to make an atonement for you before the Lord your God. For whatsoever soul it be that shall not be afflicted in that same day, he shall be cut off from among his people. And whatsoever soul it be that doeth any work in that same day, the same soul will I destroy from among his people. Ye shall do no manner of work: it shall be a statute forever throughout your generations in all your dwellings. It shall be unto you a sabbath of rest, and ye shall afflict your souls: in the ninth day of the month at even, from even unto even, shall ye celebrate your sabbath."– Leviticus 23:28-32*

The fast is sacred. The rules are explicit. You shall not work during fasting (Numbers 29:7; Leviticus 23:28-32), because the day belongs to the LORD God. Anyone living in a Jewish home, whether a believer or not, (native or foreigner), is required to join the fast. The penalty for violating the fast was fatal, *"Those who do not deny (fast) themselves on that day must be cut off from their people"* (Leviticus 23:29). As though that is not enough to portray the message, a greater emphasis is placed, *"I will destroy from among their people anyone who does any work on that day"* (Leviticus 23:30).

To the Jews, fasting is a spiritual exercise necessary for every true believer to reach spiritual unity with the Almighty.

For this we can take another pause, and ask, why do other religions fast often, but the disciples of Jesus eat and drink?

It is universally acknowledged in all religions that the entrance into the spiritual realm and high spiritual enlightenment requires fasting. If so, then why do we Christians, the disciples of Jesus disregard the imperative exercise of fasting in our spiritual walk?

Buddhism, Islam, Judaism, Taoism, Jainism, Hinduism, Scientology and every other New Age religion practice fasting as a means to spiritual enlightenment and access into the supernatural realm. Even in paganism, fasting is deemed a vital necessity in order to have active and habitual audience with the gods.

Fasting In Buddhism

It is a known fact that all the main sects of Buddhism exercise some period of fasting, especially on full-moon days and other important holidays. Fasting amongst the highly spiritual Buddhist is considered an ascetic practice, a "dhutanga" practice. (Dhutanga means "to shake up" or "invigoration"). Dhutangas is a formula for abstinent fasting and includes a specific list of thirteen practices, four of which pertain to food: eating once a day, eating at one sitting, reducing the amount you eat, on alms-round, and eating only the food that you receive at the first seven houses. These fasting practices are adopted by individual Buddhist depending on their spiritual journey. The Buddha, as is well known, emphasized moderation, the Middle Way that avoids extremes, in all things. Hence, fasting is a method the Buddhist can take up to practice spiritual moderation throughout their daily life. Among the lay community in Asia, fasting is characterized by the Chinese word "zhai" or "zai", which means at the same time "vegetarian" as well as "fasting." The point is that, for a Buddhist practitioner, removing the meat from their diet, twice a month on the new or full moon days, or six times a month, or more often, is often considered already a kind of fasting. The principle holds that removing indulgences from the diet, in this case, nutrients that are luxuries eaten to satisfy the desire for flavor, is already a form of fasting, and brings merit to the one who fasts. This will indicate that the Buddhist practitioner is involved in fasting on a daily basis.

In Buddhism, the spiritual awakening of the Buddhist is directly related to fasting. It is understood that one does not experience spiritual awakening or "mahabodhi" in Buddhism, until he or she has come out of a fast.

Fasting is fundamental in Buddhism. The founding story of the Buddhist faith relates how the Buddha was cultivating the Way in the Himalayas, having left his affluent life as a Prince of India. He sought teachers and investigated a variety of practices in his search for liberation from the suffering of old age, death and rebirth. In the course of his practices he realized that *desire* was the root of mortality. He determined, incorrectly, that if he stopped eating, he could end *desire* and gain liberation from suffering. As the story goes, he ate only a grain of rice and a sesame seed per day. Over time he got so thin that he could touch his spine by pressing on his stomach. He no longer had the strength to meditate. He realized that he would die before he understood his mind. He further realized that desire does not end by force. At that point a young herds maid offered him a meal of milk porridge which he accepted. He regained his strength, renewed his meditation, and realized Buddhahood. So, by breaking fasting and eating in moderation, he realized that the central tenet of Buddhist practice is moderation. Hence, for the Buddhist, fasting is done in moderation relative to meditation.

What puts us to shame in Christianity is that fasting for the Buddhist is a lifestyle. When a practitioner of Buddhism adopts a supervised fasting practice, he or she eats dry bread for three days to prepare the stomach for no food. The standard fasting period is eighteen days during which only a small amount of water is drunk daily. Most important is the ending of the fast, which requires small portions of thin porridge or gruel every few hours for three days, until the digestive system comes fully back to life. If this first fast is successful and beneficial to one's practice, then one can attempt a thirty-six day fast. Some fasters have extended the period gradually over years to include fasting for up to seventy-two days. This is an extreme practice that is only recommended to one who has taken all the required steps with the supervision of an experienced teacher. There's however, no doubt that the practice of fasting in Buddhism is the method to find the Way or enlightenment.

Every religion is fasting. The Muslims as we have seen fast as a means to an end. The Jews not only fast, but are commanded and required to fast. The Buddhist, to reach the high spiritual estate *"bodhi"* translated as enlightenment or self-awakening must take the journey of fasting.

Are those who practice these religions more serious about their faith than the Christian? Are they willing to set aside their stomachs for spiritual awakening and we are not? Should we, who believe we have found the true God, sacrifice less than those we consider practice false religions? Will those with a false religion offer more to their gods, and we who believe to have discovered the true God, offer less? Should their standard be higher than our standard?

Why do we not fast? Why do the disciples of Jesus not fast?

Fasting In Hinduism

We as disciples of Christ, can observe the fasting life of the Hindus as a challenge to get back to the ancient secret of fasting. There is no spiritual sojourner who was never engaged in fasting. In all of religious history, no one ever had a spiritual encounter without fasting.

The secret of fasting, as it is in other religions remains true in Hinduism. For the Hindu practitioner, fasting is commonly practiced on new moon days and during festivals such as Shivarati, Saraswati and Puja. Fasting is called *UpaVaas* in Sanskrit and Hindi. *Vaas* means staying and *Upa* means near or next to. So *UpaVaas* means staying near or next to the divine or the omnipresent, the absolute reality of the eternal. To a Christian, this will mean that fasting draws you closer to God, or creates an atmosphere in which you stay with God in close proximity.

According to the Hindu scriptures, fasting helps create harmony with the Absolute or the Brahman by establishing a perfect relationship between the body and the soul. This is thought to be imperative for the well-being of a human being as it nourishes both his or her physical and spiritual demands.

A lot of our time and energy is spent in procuring food items, preparing, cooking, eating and digesting food. Certain food types make our minds dull and agitated. Hence, the Hindu practitioner believes that on certain days man must volunteer to abstain and conserve his spiritual energy by eating either selective and light food or totally abstaining from eating so that his mind becomes alert and pure. The mind, otherwise pre-occupied by the thought of food, now entertains noble thoughts and stays with the divine or Brahman. Since it is a self-imposed form of discipline, it is usually adhered to with joy. Also, it is believed that every system needs a break and an overhaul to work at its best. During the fast, more rest and a change of diet is practiced to heal the digestive system and the entire body. The more the senses are indulged, the more they make their demands. Fasting in Hinduism is believed to help foster control over the senses, channel the desires and guide the mind to be sober and at peace.

To the Hindu practitioner, fasting should not make him or her weak, irritable or create an urge to indulge later. This happens when there is no noble goal behind fasting. The Bhagavad Gita urges to eat appropriately – neither too little nor too much, and to eat simple, pure and healthy food (a *saatvik* diet) even when not fasting.

Hindus believe it is not easy to unceasingly pursue the path of spirituality in one's daily life without fasting. Life is berated by a lot of desires, and worldly indulgences do not allow a person to concentrate on spiritual attainment. Therefore, a worshiper in Hinduism must strive to impose restraints on himself or herself to get the mind focused, and one form of such restraint is fasting. Hindus further believe that different fasts and their regulations pertaining to different gods are essentially related to the energy concentrates these divine entities are.

In Hinduism, it is believed that all gods represent a definite energy concentrate in our nature. In other words, there are different kinds of gods operating in our nature. Our nature in turn is affected by what we eat, and thereby affects the gods operating in that area of our spiritual nature. Hence, what one eats in Hinduism is specific to what god one is trying to communicate with. So, food plays the greatest role in the spiritual journey of a Hindu. You might have heard that certain Hindu gods don't like certain foods, so the practitioner must be careful regarding what they consume. By so doing the spiritual energy levels are optimally kept without any sort of interference. This is true to the old adage, *"you're what you eat."*

What's more, the fasting days are carefully chosen as it is believed that the planets and days have a direct impact on the human body. For this cause, certain fasts are to be done on specific days of the week and on certain days of the month for certain gods, based on the planetary positions in one's horoscope.

We can hence conclude that in Hinduism, one's ascension in their spiritual estate, is due to the kind of fasting they undertake. One's spiritual machoism, the highest estate of enlightenment called nirvana for the Hindu can only be attained through a dedicated habitual lifestyle of fasting.

An Appeal To The Christian

Dear Christian, the truth is that there's power in fasting. Every other religion depends on it. Every spiritual journey requires consecration by fasting and prayer. No one who desires spiritual benefits feeds on the natural. Are you in doubt that there is unfathomable power in fasting?

The challenge is yours this day. Here is an opportunity to declare such a fast as you have never engaged in before. Here is time to do it correctly as you failed to do before. The plan is to yield to Divinity; to take a pause, a spiritual hiatus, to create absolute silence in your busy daily lifestyle, and pursue a deeper relationship with God. All religious groups have tested, tried and proven that something happens when we fast.

I dare you, whether you choose to believe or not, to go on this journey. Shut yourself in. Restrict all busy schedules and movements. If need be, find a solitary place, and enter in only with your Bible in hand. Then soak yourself in it, pray with it, and read it aloud repeatedly over and over again to yourself, whilst meditating for as many days as your heart leads you. I guarantee you that Heaven will open, your eyes will open, your life will experience another place outside of this physical realm. You will either see God, or be touched by Him.

Have you ever taken a vacation from work to travel for pleasure? Have you ever taken time off from your busy schedule for a party or a ceremony? Have you ever planned fun times with your friends or loved ones? How many times have you taken time off from your busy activities so you can rest? Can you remember a day in your life, when you took some vacation from work so you can declare some days of fasting to seek God? Do you remember any day in your life when you deliberately scheduled some time for your spiritual development?

The journey begins now. It's time to pray. Let's fast. It is amazing how much time you have on your hands if you're not shopping for food, preparing it, eating it, washing the dishes, watching TV, or engaged in other pursuits. Could not this time be spent with God?

2

Their God Is Their Stomach

*Their destiny is destruction, **their god is their stomach**, and their glory is in their shame. Their mind is set on earthly things.*
– Philippians 3:19

"As it is written, Jacob have I loved, but Esau have I hated."
– Romans 9:13 –

THERE IS A CHOICE you must make between food and destiny. That choice will determine the operation of the love of God in your life. You may ask, what has food to do with God's love for me?

There is a choice that God has given humanity: Food or Destiny. There is a mysterious power in food. For the sake of destiny, do not underestimate what you eat, where you eat, when you eat and how you eat. The flesh depends on food for its survival. The Apostle Paul instructs us to be careful of the operations of the flesh, *"Because the mind of the flesh is enmity against God"* (Romans 8:7). Hence, to control the power of the flesh against the operations of God in your life, you must first control your food intake. The flesh works against the work of God in your life, and food is the fuel of the flesh. As a result, each time we eat, we are automatically empowering the flesh over the effects of God in us. Food feeds the flesh; it makes it strong; it makes the flesh pacify the spirit within.

If you are going to cultivate the power of God in your life, you must decide when to eat, and when to abstain from food.

The early church fasted habitually. For the first one thousand years of church history, it was common amongst believers to fast three times in the week. In fact, it was compulsory that every believer fast on Fridays, during those early stages of church history. The absence of habitual fasting is an indication that the modern church movement has backslidden from church precedence.

The clergy in the early church fasted on Wednesdays and Fridays. Most of our clergy of today have no such discipline and care for their spiritual estate. It is imperative for the modern church to comb its history. Often, we hear of teachings denouncing fasting as archaic, and neglecting the importance of the practice all together. Many pastors today refuse to fast. Many have never ministered on the subject of fasting throughout their entire ministerial calling.

Likewise, many believers see fasting as obsolete and as a practice buried in the church's religious history. It holds no significance to today's Christian. The church fails in fasting because the pulpit will not fast. The truth is that a pulpit that does not teach on the spiritual discipline of fasting, does not fast.

Nevertheless, Jesus, the carpenter of the Church implied in His teachings that the church would be required to fast after His ascension:

> "...But the days will come, when the bridegroom shall be taken from them, and then shall they fast." (Matthew 9:15).

Our bridegroom (Jesus Christ) ascended over two thousand years ago. But alas! We refuse to fast.

Those who God used in ages past, lived a lifestyle of fasting and prayer. The great Apostle to the Gentiles, Paul, will later voice his secret habits, "...*in fastings often*..." (2 Corinthians 11:27). The disciples of Jesus fasted weekly and in all circumstances:

> "And when they had ordained them elders in every church, and had prayed with fasting, they commended them to the Lord, on whom they believed." Acts 14:23.

The successful ministry of the early church of Jesus was characterized by prayer with fasting. Shall we offer less than their sacrifice and achieve the same results? God forbid! The standard remains the same; there are no discounts on God's blessings.

Many Christians in our churches today have gotten so busy with carnal activities that they have no time for spiritual development. We want to hear the voice of God, but we have no time to sit for it. We find ourselves eating every day, all week, months and year-round. We are eating everyday non-stop to empower the flesh against the spirit. As a result, the flesh has grown fat in pride, sinful pleasures and selfish desires. The flesh has mounted horns and is ready to destroy everything the spirit does.

Furthermore, many Christians are not growing in the things of the Spirit. The flesh has outgrown the spirit. Our desire for food is more important than our desire for God; for *"their stomach is their god."*

There is no religion on earth which does not practice fasting. Every religion on earth is established on the Law of the Fast. For this cause, child of God, you owe it to yourself to turn that plate upside down, and fast. Once in a week, or during a period within the year, it is imperative for every believer to call a personal fast and if need be, join a corporate fast.

Our destiny and spiritual relationship with God are connected to our ability to abstain from food and certain things. A detailed observation of the Genesis 3 account, illustrates the Law of the Fast, and how choosing food over destiny can destroy our posterity:

> *Now the serpent was more cunning than any beast of the field which the Lord God had made. And he said to the woman, "Has God indeed said, 'You shall not eat of every tree of the garden'?" And the woman said to the serpent, "We may eat the fruit of the trees of the garden; but of the fruit of the tree which is in the midst of the garden, God has said, 'You shall not eat it, nor shall you touch it, lest you die.' " Genesis 3:1-3*

The devil, known here as the serpent for his craftiness, appears to the woman to negotiate for the destiny of humanity. Remarkably, this was the first recorded dialogue in the Bible; and it was mysteriously centered around food. Simply put, when the enemy came to rob Adam and Eve of their destiny, he offered them food. The devil asked, *"Has God said, 'You shall not eat…?"* The woman objected, *"We may eat…"* The truth is God is not against eating. He created food, and food is nourishment for the body. As a result, God is not absolutely against our eating as the woman pointed out here. Nevertheless, we must be cautious of what we are eating, and when we are eating it. We must know that at certain times, we are to abstain from some foods. For the same God who said, "We may eat" also said, "You shall not eat." Eating then should be a selective practice for humanity. We should know when to eat, and when not to eat, and when to partially or totally abstain from eating. In sum, we should know when to fast and when not to fast. The truth here is that God expects us to fast from certain foods, at certain times.

In analyzing the conversation in Genesis 3, it is important to note why food is at the center of it all. Why must the destiny of humankind be decided around a dinner table? The devil in this story, unveils a vital fact about the significance of food: *"God knows that in the day you eat of it your eyes will be opened, and you will be like God, knowing good and evil"* (Genesis 3:5). This is a central revelation pointed out by the devil concerning God's philosophy on food. The phrase "God knows" is very revealing of the supreme effects of food in the realm of the supernatural. This is not the knowledge of normal individuals, but this is the verdict of the gods, including the Supreme Creator: "God knows". Yes, God, the Adonai, the Supreme Elohim, knows what food can do to you when you eat.

So then, we can extrapolate from the Genesis 3 account that our spiritual eyes are related to what we eat. Here, in this story, we are introduced to a type of food that opens one's spiritual eyes to uncommon knowledge immediately after consumption. This occurrence is common throughout all religions. We discovered earlier in chapter 1 that, even in Hinduism, what one eats affects their spiritual nature. The Hindus believe that food plays a significant role in how they interact with the supernatural or the tenets of the spirit world. For the Hindu, the kind of food consumed will determine which god one wants to affect or interact with.

Likewise, in the African Traditional religions, food is presented to the gods in order to gain access into the spirit world. It is common practice amongst many African traditional religions to give food to the gods. Sometimes, food is presented at the altar of the god, or in the shrine. In most cases, food is presented at the stem or roots of certain trees believed to be the gateway to the spirit world. The kind of food presented is very selective. In other words, the gods being summoned will only respond to certain kinds of foods. Amongst the Akans in Ghana (West Africa), boiled green plantain is mashed, then marinated with palm oil and some special spices. This is then garnished with boiled eggs and presented to the gods. Certain individuals, or mediums, or those who seek an audience with the spirit world may consume this food. It is common belief that your spiritual eyes will open if you eat the food prepared for the gods. Hence, this food is referred to as, "the food of the gods."

Other religions in Eastern Europe and Asia also testify to the very fact that food plays an important role in how we interact with the spirit world. Lest we forget, in Judaism as well, food is served at the altar of Jehovah in most cases. It was imperative that the Tabernacle of Moses had in it the Table of Shewbread. This was a table on which special bread was made and then presented to the Supreme Creator, known to the Jews as Yahweh. The significance of food to the gods, transcends any single religion.

Studies in Science have proven that eating certain kinds of food will open the gateway of the mind, while avoiding other kinds of food is beneficial to the eyes and mind. For example, research indicates that sugar weakens the mind, causes a reduction in brain functions, weakens memory, and increases the risk of Alzheimer and dementia. In the same light, excessive alcohol impairs the gateway to the mind, and when consumed daily is not beneficial to one's mental operation. Conclusively, Science indicates that our diet definitely has a big impact on our brain functions and our eyesight.

The compelling universal facts, in addition to the Holy Scriptures set forth that what you eat or do not eat affects your spiritual eyesight (Genesis 3:5): *"...in the day you eat of it your eyes will be opened, and you will be like God, knowing good and evil."* Biblically speaking, the food we eat is relevant to our ability to see, to be, and to know. Explicitly stated, you will see, you will be like God, and you will have supernatural knowledge, depending on the food you eat.

Many years ago, a prophet friend of mine told me to avoid eating certain kinds of food. This revelation came as we were praying. I must admit it was unorthodox, weird and bizarre. Nevertheless, as a person of faith, my spirit was in agreement with the prophetic word. For a whole year then, I went on a special kind of fast, abstaining from certain kinds of food in obedience to the prophetic direction. This strange episode changed the dynamics of my spiritual journey and prophetic abilities. After the closure of that one year fast, my spiritual eyes and senses were supernaturally activated and accentuated for spiritual things.

Whilst this may seem marvelous and startling to some, it is not out of order with the scriptures. In fact, it is a scriptural norm depicted here by the scribe:

> *"Then the eyes of both of them were opened, and they knew that they were naked; and they sewed fig leaves together and made themselves coverings."* – Genesis 3:7

When God appeared to Adam and Eve, His first inquiry to this intriguing episode was: "what did you eat?" Or "what did you eat to end up this way?"

Have you ever heard the statement, "you are what you eat?" The question you must ponder on today is, "what did you eat for your life to end up the way it now is?" Who did you eat from last night? Have you eaten of that which God said you shall not eat?

> *"Have you eaten from the tree of which I commanded you not to eat?" – Genesis 3:11*

Dear friend, it is imperative at times in your life to dedicate some time for God, and say, "I will not eat" but I will consecrate this day to seek the face of God for divine direction, for divine visitation, for divine intervention, for divine guidance, for divine protection, and above all for divine relationship.

The destiny of humanity was hanging in the balance and it was to be determined on a dining table in the restaurant of Eden (Genesis 3:1-9). The command from the eternal throne room was "thou shall not eat." The Law of the Fast was in effect. All customers were forbidden from ordering this specific meal though the chef made it desirable, pleasant, aromatic, and delicious. Yet, our first parents, Adam and Eve decided they would not fast. They would not abstain irrespective of how many lives depended on their fatal decision. They sold the destiny of humanity for a plate of food served by the devil, that ancient serpent. Just one dinner meal they said. Just a taste for today and we won't do it again tomorrow they reasoned. There, they ate away their posterity. They gave away the authority and control, the scepter of rulership delegated to them at their creation:

> *And God blessed them, and God said unto them, Be fruitful, and multiply, and replenish the earth, and subdue it: and have dominion over the fish of the sea, and over the fowl of the air, and over every living thing that moveth upon the earth. – Genesis 1:28*

Nevertheless, for a plate of food, they forfeited it all. We cannot underestimate the powerful effect that food has on us. The future of the Adamic race was tied to what they ate that day. What you eat or do not eat has an impact on your future, and the many that are queued behind you. There are too many who have exchanged their destiny over a plate of food. They couldn't fast; they couldn't abstain from that which God had forbidden, even if their destiny depended on it. The tragedy is that, like Adam and his wife, many have not only eaten away their own destinies, but they have selfishly eaten away their children's, and the destinies of their children's children from generation to generation.

The rule of life as pertaining to our eating is hereby simplified: It is not everything we are offered that we must eat, and it is not every day we must eat. Jesus puts it directly to us in this manner:

> *But he answered and said, It is written, Man shall not live by bread alone, but by every word that proceedeth out of the mouth of God. – Matthew 4:4*

Hence, sometimes it is compulsory that we eat the Word of God alone; abstaining from food in order to be with God alone. Food is not our only source of survival. We must sometimes hide ourselves, and spend time with God, eating every Word from Him.

We cannot continue to eat every day and at all times. When destiny is at stake, we must know when to abstain even if the offer of food ignites so great a desire in us. In Genesis 25, we are introduced to the tragic story of Esau, the young man who sold his entire birthright and destiny, for a bowl of stew.

His name was called Edom, because of food. The account from the scribe as recorded here is haunting and tragic:

> *"I'm starving to death! Here and now give me some of that red stew!" That's how Esau got the name "Edom.– Genesis 25:30 (CEV).*

Notice how many Christians there are today who are nicknamed by the food they love. Perhaps you are one of those, who prides yourself in your favorite food to the extent that you care not if it is used to replace your name sometimes. These are words that pierce our very soul, "Therefore his name was called Edom" (Genesis 25:30, KJV). He became a servant to his brother because of food. The scriptures declare that Esau in effect despised his birthright (the right to his destiny). He sold it for a bowl of stew. He gave away destiny for a five-minute meal.

Dear friend, may you not be like Esau. You have a choice before you today: Food or Destiny. The choice is yours to make. Will you set apart some time now to fast, pray and consecrate yourself to God? Or will you be like Esau, who when presented with the choice, said:

> "Behold, I am at the point to die: and what profit shall this birthright do to me?" (Genesis 25:32).

This Esau could not sacrifice for his destiny. He could not abstain for one day. However, like Esau, there are many believers, perhaps you included, who cannot go a day without food. They will rather sacrifice destiny for that one meal.

Oh, child of God, remember Esau and fast. It was this action of his that perhaps provoked the Omniscient eyes of God through time to prophesy saying:

> (For the children being not yet born, neither having done any good or evil, that the purpose of God according to election might stand, not of works, but of him that calleth;). It was said unto her, The elder shall serve the younger. As it is written, Jacob have I loved, but Esau have I hated. – Romans 9:11-13

Is it not possible that God made this executive decision, "Jacob have I loved, but Esau have I hated" because He foresaw Esau's choice? God knew Esau would despise his birthright. God knew Esau would choose a bowl of food over his destiny. It was the Omniscient knowledge that automatically resulted in the divine selection between the two brothers.

The love God had for Jacob was based on his decision to abstain from food: "Jacob have I loved."

The Law of the Fast, is to put God above food (the desire of the flesh). Food is a mysterious fuel to the carnal person. It is true that if you want to know what is in the heart of a person, feed them food. Take them to dinner at a good restaurant and if care is not taken, they will spill out the deepest secrets in their heart without persuasion. When food is in front of people, they'll talk without realizing they're talking. They'll not stop talking when the food is good. The more the food, the more they'll give away all their hidden secrets.

Remember, men take women on a date over food. Have you asked yourself why? In marriage, food is known to be tantamount to sex; a good meal could force a man quickly into bed with a woman. It is said, "the way to a man's heart is through his stomach." High profile business meetings sometimes happen around a lunch date. Important contracts have been signed by corporations and individuals at top-notch restaurants and not in cozy offices. In the process of eating, someone's mind is being inculcated. Someone is selling their soul at the dinner table. Someone is exchanging their destiny for a delicious tenderloin steak.

What's more, food plays a supreme role in our decision making and destiny. Food is a requisite to life; it is required for humanity's survival. That is why when someone abstains from food for God, there is an explosive release of divine blessings. As we turn our bowls upside down to fast, and seek the presence of God, may we experience divine visitation and angelic entertainments.

3

Repairer of the Breach

"And they that shall be of thee shall build the old waste places: thou shalt raise up the foundations of many generations; and thou shalt be called, The Repairer of the Breach, The Restorer of paths to dwell in" – Isaiah 58:12

WHENEVER I THINK of a breach, it is either a breach of a contract or the breaching of a city wall by an army. God's Word covers several meanings for breach.

- **Breach** (Dictionary): An opening made by breaking down something solid; gap; alienation;

estrangement; to take the place of someone missing, or unable to act in an emergency. A breaking of a promise

- **Breach** (Bible) A bursting forth or breach; transgression, breach of trust or to break open
- **Repair** (Dictionary): To put into good condition again; to mend; to make up for or remedy
- **Repair** (Bible): To renew, restore or healing and restoration.

Exodus 22:9 records:

> *For every breach of trust, whether it is for ox, for donkey, for sheep, for clothing, or for any lost thing about which one says, 'This is it,' the case of both parties shall come before the judges; he whom the judges condemn shall pay double to his neighbor. (NASB)*

Yahweh took a strong stand on a breach of trust. In the Exodus account, the breach would be taking what does not belong to you.

> *They made a calf in Horeb, And worshiped the molded image. Thus they changed their glory Into the image of an ox that eats grass. 21 They forgot God their Savior, Who had done great things in Egypt, Wondrous works in the land of Ham, Awesome things by the Red Sea. Therefore He said that He would destroy them, Had not Moses His chosen one stood before Him in the breach, To turn away His wrath, lest He destroy them. – Psalm 106:19-23 (NKJV)*

This breach was a place where Moses stood between God and Israel to intercede. Had Moses not stepped in, God's wrath would have gone forth and destroyed the entire nation! In fact, God told Moses that He would use Moses to create new nation.

In the Book of Isaiah, we see another side of a "breach": that of restoration and repair.

> *Then you shall call, and the LORD will answer; You shall cry, and He will say, 'Here I am.' " If you take away the yoke from your midst, The pointing of the finger, and speaking wickedness, [10] If you extend your soul to the hungry And satisfy the afflicted soul, Then your light shall dawn in the darkness, And your darkness shall be as the noonday. The LORD will guide you continually, And satisfy your soul in drought, And strengthen your bones; You shall be like a watered garden, And like a spring of water, whose waters do not fail. Those from among you Shall build the old waste places; You shall raise up the foundations of many generations; <u>And you shall be called the Repairer of the Breach, The Restorer of Streets to Dwell In</u>. – Isaiah 58:9-12 (NKJV)*

This is an important view of breaching. Yahweh indicts His people for their self-centered, selfish approach to life and to fasting. He points out that there is a proper way to fasting that can lead to a place pleasing to the Lord! It revolves around a choice to invest into peoples' lives through a change of heart, as opposed to wearing sackcloth and ashes for an outward fast! God reveals their hearts to demonstrate what they were actually doing and not what they thought they were doing.

> *'Why have we fasted,' they say, 'and you have not seen it? Why have we humbled ourselves, and you have not noticed?' "Yet on the day of your fasting, you do as you please and exploit all your*

> *workers. Your fasting ends in quarreling and strife, and in striking each other with wicked fists. You cannot fast as you do today and expect your voice to be heard on high.* – Isaiah 58:3-4 (NIV)

OK, so can we be actual "repairers of the breach"? Absolutely! It is a matter of intercession coupled with action. <u>There are so many breaches today</u>. God can use us to repair these breaches and His repair is focused on renewal, restoration and healing. It is what Jesus would have us do. We can easily choose or find breaches that need repair.

A breach is "a break or a gap in a fence, hedge, or wall." Walls or fences were constructed for protection and preservation. Boundaries were hedged to preserve property lines, and towns were walled to protect from enemies. When these walls were broken, eroded, or allowed to deteriorate, it caused breaches or gaps, and a breakdown of protection. Someone would have to repair the breaches or the occupants would be in great jeopardy.

In every generation, "repairers of the breach" have been greatly needed, and they are certainly needed today. Walls of protection and separation have suffered great damage. Compromise and disobedience have eroded the hedges that ought to protect. We have witnessed an all-out assault on the protective walls of our family units, our churches, and our nation. Moral walls have been greatly damaged.

Attacks on traditional marriage, opposition to public references to God, and legalized abortion are examples. The hedges around the Lord's churches have been weakened by worldliness, ecumenism, and rejection of Biblical truth. The safe haven of families has been breached through similar matters of compromise and disobedience. The spiritual protection of the individual can be removed by willful sin and by giving ground to the enemy.

To restore the protection, the breaches must be repaired. How can we rebuild the walls around our lives and ministries? Through repentance, obedience, and intercession, we can see these hedges rebuilt. The number of those who are determined to see the old landmarks removed continues to grow. We must be just as committed to the cause of following the old paths of obedience and godliness. As such, we too can be called "repairers of the breach."

The Scripture in Isaiah 58 really describes our culture. It is one of self-centeredness, greed and the breaking of covenants. We desperately need to stand in intercession as Moses did, before God sends forth His wrath. The foundations our nation was built upon are still there, but they are badly eroded. We can indeed, through prayer, restore the Godly foundations of many past generations. As we look at the old, grand church buildings, we should pause for a moment and reflect on the people who constructed them and walked out their covenant relationship with our Lord. These structures were built at a great cost and were meant to be places of worship and of the preaching of the Word. Yet, sadly, many preachers have fallen away and the Word has been diluted. As He leads, we need to continue to ask God to restore our churches.

As I read and reread this Scripture, my heart is deeply touched. There are many Christians who have been hurt by words and actions done in the name of Jesus Christ. Breaches have been opened in their lives and they are struggling greatly to re-establish direction and faith. They have seen trust broken both in fellowship and in leadership, and some have left the very fellowship needed in their lives. However, we can be there for them to minister to them and help them find their way back. God's love is able to repair those breaches! As we remain faithful to His Word and intercede, we will see God bring people to us for the healing of these hurts.

> *"And they that shall
> be of thee shall build
> the old waste places:
> thou shalt raise up the
> foundations of many
> generations; and thou
> shalt be called, The
> Repairer of the
> Breach,
> The Restorer of paths
> to dwell in"*
>
> – Isaiah 58:12

Who are these people? Can you become one of them? The answer is: every believer can.

> *"And they shall build the old wastes, they shall raise up the former desolations, and they shall repair the waste cities, the desolations of many generations." - Isaiah 61:4*

1) A breach is a break or gap in a wall or fence. Through it the enemy can come in and through it the innocent may wander off and be lost.

2) Repairing spiritual breaches is the responsibility of all believers, especially that of the priesthood. The Almighty will withhold His blessings from you if you fail to do your duty.

3) No matter what your profession: (priest, ruler, doctor, engineer, fitness trainer, teacher - man or woman) you can become a Repairer of the Breach, a Restorer of paths to dwell in.
But expect opposition, because the enemy of souls is never pleased when "breaches are being

repaired," or when the "old paths are being restored."

4) It is absolutely essential that only the finest of materials be used; Yahweh's truth, His law and His Word. Only these must be used. We cannot use our *"personal opinions," "human traditions," "ocult practices," "human psychology or the sciences of this world"* to restore the breaches. Like untempered mortar, these will never stand the test of divine Judgement.

5) We can compare false prophets to bogus builders. In the time of trouble their flimsy structures and vain prophecies will collapse in ruins.

6) Many Spiritual Breaches have been made in the Almighty's property: *marriage,* the *holy Sabbath day,* the *law of God,* and the *authentic Word of God.* All have been broken into, vandalized and mutilated. Let us restore them to their former glory. If we do this conscientiously, we will be called 'Repairers of the Breach,' the 'Restorers of paths to dwell in.'

Notice the Scripture does not say that Yahweh is the one who would repair the breach. Instead the Scripture here says we are the ones who must repair and restore. It is our job to seek the Face of the LORD; it is our job to know the Word and proclaim the Truth of God's Word.

As we journey through this fasting experience, let us always remember that there is a calling on us to go where there are breaches.

Oh LORD God, may we always be known as "repairers of the breach" and the restorers of paths to dwell in! May You be glorified in all we do.

4

How To Begin

As you begin your fast, you may hear from concerned loved ones and friends who urge you to protect your health. They are right. You should protect your health. But I assure you, if done properly, fasting will not only prove to be a spiritual blessing, but also a physical blessing as well.

Types of Fasting

1. **The Normal Fast:** In this type of fast the person abstains from food but not from water. The duration can be that which the individual or group feels led to

set. Jesus fasted for 30 days (Matthew 4:2). However, the more common practice of a normal fast is from one to three days.

2. **The Partial Fast:** In this type of fast, the emphasis is placed on restriction of diet, rather than abstaining completely from eating. Examples are: Daniel, Shadrack, Meshach and Abednego eating only vegetables and drinking only water (Daniel 1:15), and later on when Daniel alone practiced a Partial Fast for three weeks (Daniel 10:3). The Partial Fast allows for many variations:

   o Variation 1 - Exclusively specific types of food for the duration of the fast. For example fruits and vegetables, plain bread and water, plain rice, or juices. We are recommending a fresh fruit and vegetable juice fast for those who want to take the challenge.

   o Variation 2 - Omitting a certain meal each day and spending that meal time with the Lord. (Care is needed to ensure that the value of omitting one meal is not offset by increasing intake at the others).

3. **The Absolute Fast:** An Absolute Fast is one in which the person refrains from both food and water. This type of fast is not to exceed three days. Exceptions to this three day limit (1 Kings 19:8; Deuteronomy 9:9-18 and Exodus 34:28) were based upon direct, divine guidance and care. Examples of participants in the Absolute Fast are: Moses (Deuteronomy 9:9-18 and Exodus 34:28); Elijah (1 Kings 19:8); Ezra (Ezra 10:6); Esther and her household (Esther 4:16); and Paul (Acts 9:9).

Fasting cleanses the body and refreshes the soul. During a fast the body cleanses, purifies and essentially resurrects itself. Nature tells us to fast. When we have no appetite during an illness, fasting is nature's way to accelerate recovery. Fasting is NOT starvation. It is reasonable for a healthy individual to fast for 2 or 3 days without supervision.

Fifteen Ways To Fast

1) No meals except water for 30 days.
2) One meal of juices a day for 30 days.
3) One meal of food a day for 30 days.
4) No meals (except water), three days per week for the entire 30 days.
5) No meals (except water), one day per week, for the entire 30 days.
6) Daniel Fast: Only eat nuts, grains, fruits, and vegetables for 30 days.
7) All juice and drink water only, three days per week for the entire 30 days.
8) All meal fast for half of the 30 days.
9) Simply greens and water for 30 days.
10) Fast away breakfast for 30 days.
11) Bread and water (or milk) for 30 days.
12) Television, Instagram, Video games, Facebook, or other social websites for 30 days (for children).
13) Junk food, desserts, sweets, soft drinks, or chocolate for 30 days (for children).
14) No meals for 7 days, 2 meals a day for next 7 days,

1 meal a day for the rest of the Fast.
15) Fasting away from specific foods by revelation for 30 days (I had a revelation to fast away from peppers, meat, dairy products, and salt for 9 months).

A Message To Families About Prayer And Fasting Together

Your children may hear you speak about your prayer and fasting with much anticipation. They may wonder if this is something that they can do along with their family, and the answer is yes! Explain to your children that fasting will help them grow stronger as a Christian and closer to Jesus. When they take special time out to pray to Jesus and at the same time, take special effort to not enjoy a favorite food or snack item or activity during a certain period of time, they are fasting. As a family, sit down together and talk about for whom or what your children are seeking God, and how they are going to fast. Then, have your children write down their decisions, just as you will, and seal it in a self-addressed envelope with no names on it. We will collect the sealed envelopes during our prescribed services. There will be times when your children will find it hard to fast and may even want to change their minds in the middle of the fast. However, as parents, gently encourage them and help them to keep the commitment they made to the Lord, and to see how He answers their prayers. Following the 30 days of fasting and praying, sit down with them and talk about what the Lord did during this special time. As a family, use the 30th day to break the fast together at a special evening gathering at home.

Moreover, before you begin the 30-day fasting, keep in mind your family's schedule and decide which days of the week you are going to meet together to pray. Be sure to explain in simple words the prayer emphasis for that particular day, so your children can be a part of the prayer time.

Remember that a child's body needs the proper nutrition and activity, as well as rest to keep them healthy and whole. They don't need to fast complete meals or healthy food choices for days at a time, or give up the exercise that playtime affords. Children respond best with a set schedule, so be sure to create one in which they will know which days during the 30 days of prayer and fasting they will be fasting and what exactly they are fasting.

FORMAT: The 30-Day Fasting Guide

WHEN: If fasting alone, you must prayerfully decide, and plan the fasting period as you'd plan a vacation. This will give you the opportunity to spend useful time with God. If fasting with a church, follow the guidelines of your leadership and do not stray from the structure of the corporate fast.

WHY: That we might humble ourselves before our God and ask Him for guidance, protection and to open doors for us, our children, all our lineage, our community and our nation. You must always have an objective to fast. Read Isaiah 58 for proper guidance on your objective. If fasting with a church, follow the objective of the church fast.

HOW: From 12 twilight to 6:00 p.m., drink only water for the entire duration of the fast. It is better to warm your water, and add pure honey, when possible. You may nourish yourself with prescribed foods between the hours of 6:00 p.m. to 12:00 twilight. See food guidelines below. Also restrict your media, communications, and entertainment activities to necessity. It is beneficial to use those leisure times for your personal Bible Study. Listen to Bible on Audio. A good preaching on the subject of fasting and pursuing God will be great as the occasion presents itself. Also listen to devotional worships and praises to stir up your spirit to pray earnestly. The above time structure is only a recommendation. The time period for your fasting may change if you're on an absolute fast. If you're on needed medications, or are involved in other intense activities, you may choose to wisely break the fast earlier at around 3:00 p.m., or by advice of a doctor or pastor.

FORMAT: We recommend that you follow "The Daniel Fast Principle." Meals are to consist of wholesome foods. The Daniel Fast Principle is chosen as a norm for most fasting, but you may prayerfully choose which fast you will do.

READINGS: Isaiah 58: Please read the entire chapter as a devotional. We will be focusing on this entire chapter of Isaiah for the duration of the fast. Please read carefully the entire chapter before beginning the Fast. Other scriptures are provided in this guide on a day by day digest.

HELPS: Visit our website for additional resources or email us. Visit www.prayercell.com or email info@prayercell.com for further assistance.

BREAKING THE FAST
BETWEEN 6:00 PM TO 12:00AM Twilight

Please be sure to **READ THE LABEL** when purchasing packaged, canned or bottled foods. They should be **sugar-free** and **chemical-free**. Keep this in mind as you review this list of acceptable foods. Fasting is a deliberate choice to avoid certain things, so be deliberate when picking what to eat.

CHOICE OF FOOD: The Daniel Fast Principle

All Fruits (fresh, frozen, dried, juiced, or canned): including but are not limited to - apples, apricots, bananas, blackberries, blueberries, boysenberries, cantaloupes, cherries, cranberries, figs, grapefruits, grapes, guavas, honeydew melons, kiwis, mangoes, nectarines, papayas, peaches, pears, pineapples, plums, prunes, raisins, raspberries, strawberries, tangelos, tangerines, and watermelons.

All Vegetables (fresh, frozen, dried, juiced, or canned): including but are not limited to - artichokes, asparagus, beets, broccoli, brussels sprouts, cabbage, carrots, cauliflower, celery, chili peppers, collard greens, corn, cucumbers, eggplant, garlic, ginger root, kale, leeks, lettuce, mushrooms, mustard greens, okra, onions, parsley, potatoes, radishes, rutabagas, scallions, spinach, sprouts, squashes, sweet potatoes, tomatoes, turnips, watercress, yams, zucchini, and veggie burgers (optional) if you are not allergic to soy.

All Whole Grains: including but not limited to – whole wheat, brown rice, millet, quinoa, oats, barley, grits, whole wheat pasta, whole wheat tortillas, rice cakes, and popcorn.

All Legumes (canned or dried): including but not limited to - dried beans, pinto beans, split peas, lentils, black-eyed peas, kidney beans, black beans, cannellini beans, and white beans.

All Nuts and Seeds: including but are not limited to – sunflower seeds, cashews, peanuts, and sesame. Also nut butters including peanut butter.

All Quality Oils: including but not limited to – Olive, canola, grape seed, peanut, and sesame.

Beverages: Spring water, distilled water, or other pure waters.

Other: Tofu, soy products, vinegar, seasonings, salt, herbs, and spices.

Foods to Avoid on the Fast

All meat and animal products including but not limited to – beef, lamb, pork, poultry, and fish.

All dairy products including but not limited to - milk, cheese, cream, butter, and eggs.

All sweeteners including but not limited to – sugar, raw sugar, syrups, molasses, and cane juice.

All refined and processed foods products including but not limited to – artificial flavorings, food additives, chemicals, white rice, white flour, and foods that contain artificial preservatives.

All deep fried foods including but not limited to – potato chips, french fries, corn chips.

All solid fats including but not limited to – shortening, margarine, lard, and foods high in fat.

Beverages including but not limited to – coffee, teas (with stimulants, including black tea and herbal tea with stimulants), carbonated beverages, energy drinks, and alcohol.

Acidic fruits, including but not limited to – orange juices, oranges, lemon or lime, grape juices.

Suggested Daily Guide For Juice Fast

If you are beginning a juice fast, there are certain juices you may wish to avoid and certain ones that are especially beneficial. You may find the following daily schedule helpful during your fast:

- 5:00 a.m. - 8:00 a.m.
  Fruit juices, preferably freshly squeezed or blended, diluted in 50 percent distilled water if the fruit is acidic. Orange, apple, pear, grapefruit, papaya, grape, peach or other fruits are good.

- 10:30 a.m. - noon
  Vegetable juice made from lettuce, celery, and carrots in three equal parts.

- 2:30 p.m. - 4:00 p.m.
  Herb tea OR simply hot water with a drop of honey. Make sure that it is not black tea or tea with a stimulant.

- 6:00 p.m. - 8:30 p.m.
  Broth from boiled potatoes, celery, and carrots (no salt).

I suggest that you do not drink diary milk because it is a pure food and therefore a violation of the fast. Any product containing protein or fat, such as milk or soy-based drinks, should be avoided depending on the kind of fast you choose to enter. Be advised these products will restart the digestion cycle and you will again feel hunger pangs. Also, for health reasons, stay away from caffeinated beverages such as coffee, tea, or cola. Because caffeine is a stimulant, it has a more powerful effect on your nervous system when you abstain from food. This works both against the physical and spiritual aspects of the fast.

Another key factor in maintaining optimum health during a fast is to limit your physical activity. Exercise only moderately, and rest as much as your schedule will permit (this especially applies to extended fasts). Short naps are helpful as well. Walking a mile or two each day at a moderate pace is acceptable for a person in good health, and on a juice fast. However, no one on a water fast should exercise without the supervision of a fasting specialist.

How To Finish Your Fast In A Healthy Way

Most experts agree that breaking a fast with vegetables, either steamed or raw, is best. Your stomach is smaller at this point, so eat lightly. Stop before you feel full. Stay away from starches like pastas, potatoes, rice, or bread (except for "Melba toast"). Also avoid meats, dairy products, and any fats or oils. Introduce them slowly and in small amounts.

Extended fasts are not the only fasts which need to be ended with caution. Even a 3-day fast requires reasonable precautions. It is wise to start with a little soup - one which is thin and nourishing, such as vegetable broth made from onion, celery, potatoes, and carrots - and fresh fruits such as watermelon and cantaloupe.

In terms of resuming any sort of exercise routine, the advice is the same. Start out slowly, allowing time for your body to re-adjust to its usual regimen.

Pre-Fast Caution

1. DO NOT BEGIN YOUR FAST SUDDENLY The body grows accustomed to fasting by degrees.
2. Reduce food intake gradually from three times a day to two times, then once a day, and into the fast.
3. Clean the digestive tract prior to fasting. Some recommend the last meal before a fast to be fruits. A person who has problems with constipation should take an enema.
4. Cease taking coffee or tea a few days before a longer fast, in order to get over the caffeine- withdrawal headache before you start.

During The Fast

1. Drink water (preferably distilled or boiled warm water with a pinch of salt). Be careful not to drink too much water at one time. A glass or so several times a day is ideal. One should not drink milk or coffee or other beverages when fasting for to do so is dieting and not fasting. Water is a purifying agent, and is necessary to wash out the poisons from the system.
2. Drink fruit and vegetable juices. They are full of nutrients, provide instant nutrition and are rapidly absorbed by the body.
- Fruit juices are energizers and body cleansers. Dilute with water because fruit juices are high in natural sugar

and when ingested without diluting with water during a prolonged fast could make you feel a little dizzy.
- Mixing and matching too many fruit juices during a prolonged fast will only put unnecessary strain on the digestive system. The common recommendation is to mix apple with any of these fruits: grapefruit, mango, peaches, guava, kiwi, papaya, pear. All melons (honeydew, rock melon, watermelon) should be taken alone.
- Vegetable juices are building blocks supplying the body with the necessary vitamins and minerals to build strong bones and tissues. Mix with cucumber, carrots or apples or dilute with water and take in small quantities (1 cup) to avoid any discomfort.
- All juices should be sipped slowly.
- Anyone who has to limit sugar intake in their diet should consume fruit juices sparingly. The common recommendation is not more than 500 ml spread throughout a week and be sure to follow your doctor's instructions.

3. Refrain from taking an excessively hot bath. Having a very hot bath during a prolonged fast can cause dizziness, and you may be unable to continue. Instead bathe in lukewarm water. It is important to bathe regularly during a fast as many impurities are secreted through the pores of the skin and cause a foul odor. Also be sure to brush your teeth often as fasting produces bad

breath.
4. Do not engage in excessive work or exercise. Some light exercise (eg. walking) is beneficial. Reading the Bible during a fast is a necessity and spiritually beneficial.
5. Walk, read, pray or worship Christ at mealtimes to help overcome the great temptation to satisfy the eating instinct. If possible, avoid looking at food and coming to the table at meal times. If you remain where eating is taking place, the temptation to break the fast will be very great.

Symptoms During a Prolonged Fast:

1. Possible dizziness. Do not jump out of bed quickly. Get off your feet and lie down immediately if you begin to feel light-headed at any time.
2. Vomiting may occur during the first few days and is normal.
3. Headaches are occasionally experienced early in the first day or two of fasting. However, most people with a history of severe headaches or migraines may find that this disappears as the fast continues.
4. Generally, the need for sleep is greatly

diminished when we are not active and when our digestive tract is not at work digesting food. It is an added risk to drink coffee during a prolonged fast.

5. Weight loss is to be expected. Possible weakness, nervousness, slight trembling, irritability, negativity, frequent urination and sometimes diarrhea may occur but these are usually only temporary. The body is undergoing a cleansing and elimination process and as the poisons are eliminated any symptoms will disappear.

6. Never have an injection or take medicine or massive doses of vitamins to alleviate these symptoms. Instead, drink as much fluid in between the juices as possible. Should you experience any major discomfort consult your doctor for advice.

7. Many people do not generally have bowel movements during a fast. Eat primarily raw fruits and vegetables for a few days prior to the fast to help prevent difficulty with the first bowel movement afterward.

8. During a prolonged fast, the body goes through 3 phases. They are not always clearly defined, but tend to overlap, and the duration of each varies greatly with the individual.

- First phase - craving for food. This may last for a couple of days or longer. Once it passes though, there may be a pleasurable sensation at the thought of food and there is no craving or strong temptation.

- Second phase - feeling of weakness and faintness which may last for 2 or 3 days or much longer. At this point, every movement of the body seems to require an effort of the will. This is the most difficult part of the fast, and some may find it necessary to rest a good deal.

- Third phase - one of growing strength, with little or no concern about food and only occasional and decreasing spasms of weakness. At this stage, the person fasting often feels he could continue the fast indefinitely without any great effort. The termination of this final phase is marked by the beginning of hunger pangs and this is a warning bell that the body is beginning to starve. It is important to distinguish between a desire for food and a hunger for food. The sensations of emptiness, weakness, gnawing in the pit of the stomach and other symptoms experienced at the onset of a fast are seldom real hunger. Real hunger, on the other hand, is a cry from the whole body stemming not from habit but from need. Humans have been fasting for thousands of years. It is hard to understand how people developed such a misconception about and fear of fasting. Perhaps it is because many people feel so bad when they skip just one meal that they expect to feel much worse if they skip many more. The reality is, when you don't eat for a longer period of time, the discomfort quickly subsides and you actually feel better and better.

DAY 1
Hypocrisy

Cry aloud, spare not, lift up thy voice like a trumpet, and shew my people their transgression, and the house of Jacob their sins. – (Isaiah 58:1)

DAY 1 – Hypocrisy

Today is the first day of something new. Regardless of where you are in your relationship with God, 30 days of prioritizing the Lord over essential needs in your life will draw you closer to Him and transform whatever needs to change. So today pray that God will help you to envision how you will resemble Him more closely at the end of these 30 days.

LOG-ON: DAY 1 – Morning Prayers

Give glory and adoration to God. Confess your sins before Him and receive the assurance and surety of forgiveness in the mercies of the divine blood of Jesus. Now continue your prayer in this suggested manner, and spend at least five minutes on each of these prayer points:

1. Under the covering of the Superior Blood of Jesus, I confess, believe and declare that Jesus Christ is my LORD, Master, and Savior. I forfeit all ties with my sinful nature and plead the exemption of the superior blood against impending judgment ordained for my sins and trespasses.
2. Under the covering of the Superior Blood of Jesus, LORD give me strength in my weakness, sustain me with your Spirit divine, and break every yoke and bondage of immorality in my life in Jesus' name.
3. Under the covering of the Superior Blood of Jesus, I escape every arrow of diabolical influence to blindfold me and lead me into sin, the lust of the flesh, and to make me a prisoner to lies, gossip, backbiting, and blackmailing, in Jesus' name.
4. Under the covering of the Superior Blood of Jesus, I unleash the superior blood of Jesus against any negative dreams, attacks against my vision, my desires and destiny, in Jesus' name.

5. Under the covering of the Superior Blood of Jesus, have mercy upon me, O God, according to thy loving-kindness. According unto the multitude of thy tender mercies blot out my transgressions.
6. Under the covering of the Superior Blood of Jesus, my Father, create in me a clean heart, O God, and renew a right spirit within me.
7. Under the covering of the Superior Blood of Jesus, LORD, restore unto me the joy of thy salvation, and uphold me with thy free spirit.
8. Under the covering of the Superior Blood of Jesus, I receive the unction to function today and to be an overcomer, in Jesus' name.
9. Under the covering of the Superior Blood of Jesus Christ, I am unreservedly committed to my local church, the services, vision, purpose and plans. For me, there is no such thing as partial commitment again.
10. Under the covering of the Superior Blood of Jesus Christ, my commitment is final and I have stopped making excuses and this is deciding and defining my future for the better.

DAY 1

Hypocrisy

Cry aloud, spare not, lift up thy voice like a trumpet, and shew my people their transgression, and the house of Jacob their sins. – (Isaiah 58:1)

YAHWEH IS CALLING FOR OUR ATTENTION. The demand here is for the restoration of a broken relationship between God and His people. It is easy to count the sins of others, but the question should be, "Am I right with God?" A genuine self-examination is required here: "God, are my hands clean?". A deeper search of my own soul is in question here: *"Search me, O God, and know my heart: try me, and know my thoughts: And see if there be any wicked way in me, and lead me in the way everlasting."* (Psalm 139:23-24)." Another translation of this cry of the psalmist is more provoking: *"Look deep into my heart, God, and find out everything I am thinking"* (Psalm 139:23 CEV). Have you ever thought about the fact that God knows everything you are thinking? Even that evil thought you had against someone who walked into church? That thought in you that makes you think you are better than the other person? That thought that tells you that you are holier and more spiritual than the next person? If God does the searching, He will not miss any debris of sins in you.

Have you ever paused to ask yourself, "if God is to do a deep searching in my heart, what will He find?" The highly sophisticated hi-tech, x-ray scanners in the airports are able to search and detect any illegal substance or weapon as you walk through. Now, ponder upon the eyes of the Most High, scanning your heart, gazing into the depths of your soul and spirit, what will He find? The greatest prayer we can all pray is "Search me, O God, and know my heart…see if there be any wickedness in me."

As we enter this fast, we first approach the throne to examine our relationship with God. What time do I give to God? Is God my priority? Am I seeking the Kingdom of God, and His righteousness first? Will I make Heaven if I am to die today? Am I truly saved?

In today's culture, we do not have time for church, prayer, and personal devotion. Our prayer life is in a haste. We pray whilst we're showering; we pray whilst we are driving; we pray whilst we are cooking; we pray whilst doing everything and there's scarcely time for just prayer with nothing else. We call this "activity prayer". This kind of praying is good, but it must be done as an addition to our "quiet time" with God. The Christian must find time to sit, shut-off everything, and give God all their attention.

We also have those amongst us, who do not find time to pray at all. They wake up each morning, take their shower, take a bite at their breakfast, and quickly run outside to catch the transportation to work. In like manner, they close from work, run home tired, eat their dinner, and lackadaisically sit to watch television, until they are ready to fall asleep. They have no appetite to even share a five-minute prayer before bed.

Yet, these are the first to lament, and curse at God when their lives are not going right. There are many who are embittered with church and fellow Christians, but they will not first examine their own hearts. O Child of God, is your heart right with God? Is there a genuine relationship with Him in your life?

In this first verse of Isaiah 58, God has a problem with us. He sent His representative, the Prophet Isaiah to give us the divine indictment: *"Cry aloud, spare not, lift thy voice like a trumpet..."* (v.1a).

We first examine God's charge to the prophet here, "cry aloud".

This word "cry" is from the Hebrew word "qara" which means to call, cry, utter a loud sound, or to proclaim.

This charge to the prophet by God demands some attention from us, especially from a church age where loud preaching is demeaned and frowned upon. The church today is shifting toward an atmosphere that is dry, dreary, and spiritually dreadful. The preacher is not allowed to "lift up" his or her voice as it may be seen as "screaming at the people" or offensive. But here we find God, pressing the prophet to deliver this message with the full-force of his voice: "cry aloud". What we need today are courageous, unabashed preachers who can cry aloud against the sins of the modern believer.

The word "aloud" in the Hebrew is "garown", which means neck or throat. If the prophet is to get the people's attention, he must shout – "call with the throat," which means to preach with full voice.

The prophet or the preacher must not hesitate to enforce God's Word against sin. The charge from Heaven is, "spare not," which in the Hebrew (chasak) means not to withhold, restrain, hold back, or refrain. This means we must be forceful in our fight against sin. God does not entertain sin, neither should you. It is an insult to God for you to be sinning whilst you are fasting. It is a breach to hold unforgiveness in your heart whilst asking God to forgive you and bless you.

In this season of fasting, do not entertain sin. God is absolutely and rigorously against sin of any kind. God will not bless sin. Yahweh is shouting loud against sin everyday in the life of the believer. Hence, we must also lift up our voices, like trumpets (Hebrew: sopars or shawphars) against sin. We must forcefully hate, and denounce sin in our lives, in our brethren, in the church and in the world. The word trumpet here is the Hebrew translation "sopar," which is a ram's horn, an instrument that could be used rather like a bugle to call soldiers to assembly or to battle. Blowing the trumpet was the best way to get people's attention.

Why is God so eager to call our attention? What has caused Yahweh to be so heartbroken that He needs to urgently send a prophet to lament with such force?

If you are wondering what God is most concerned about in your life, lets hear it in His own words:

> "...shew my people their transgression, and the house of Jacob their sins." (Isaiah 58:1b)

Sin is God's biggest problem with us. And the worst sin is the "nonchalant sin"; the sin committed so casually that we do not even care what God thinks. The prophet was sent to point out the sins of Israel, because the people pretended to be blind to the consequences of their sinful actions.

Moreover, the reason why Yahweh is calling our attention is to announce our hypocrisy aloud – to bring to awareness that hidden sin. The sin of hypocrisy is often kept in the dark. In fact, it is hard for us to genuinely detect that we are hypocrites in certain circumstances and with some individuals.

In this fasting day, you must pray the prayer, "search me O Yahweh, look deep into my heart, and find out what I am thinking." If you search yourself, you will miss most of the hidden sins in the darkest corners of your soul, but if Yahweh searches you, His eyes are more powerful than any x-ray machine; all is exposed that needs to be disposed of.

⇒ **TIPS FOR THE DAY**

Avoid Calling Attention to your Fasting & Prayer (Isaiah 58 verse 1)

- Avoid drawing attention to yourself during a fast so that everyone gets the impression that you're fasting. Don't go around parading to everyone or anyone that you're in a fast. This is between you and God and not to give the imprint of spiritual machismo and also not for applause from fellow saints.

- Nevertheless, do not behave as though this is a secret mission that no one including your spouse or roommate must know about. This parallel behavior can create confusion within relationships. Advise your partner that you're in a fast to avoid any confusion related to not eating prepared meals and resisting marital intercourse.

-

PRAYER GUIDE 1:

- Pray and humbly confess your sins to the LORD and repent of all trespasses.
- Pray consecrating yourself for the LORD to sanctify you.
- Pray against the spirit of pride, that the LORD will preserve your tongue and deeds.
- Pray for gifts of wisdom and knowledge as you enter this fasting season.
- Pray for the spiritual gift of discerning of other spirits as you come into the fast.

LOG-OFF: DAY 1 - Evening Prayers

Give glory and adoration to the King of Glory and take refuge in the blood of Jesus Christ as you enter this prayer. Spend at least five minutes on each of these prayer points:

1. Thank you Lord for calling me to a deeper commitment to you and making me conscious of the need to commit myself and mine to you.
2. Under the covering of the Superior Blood of Jesus Christ, I hereby confess that I am leaving all and everything to follow you, for nothing is as important to me as you.
3. Under the covering of the Superior Blood of Jesus Christ, LORD, I have faith in you and so without any hesitation I have turned everything about my life over to you for you know best.
4. Under the covering of the Superior Blood of Jesus Christ, LORD, I am yielded and surrendered to you and your will.
5. Under the covering of the Superior Blood of Jesus Christ, LORD, I present myself, as your obedient child, whose all-consuming passion is to do your will. I know I am not my own anymore for I am bought with a price.
6. Under the covering of the Superior Blood of Jesus Christ, I am separated from the world and its lusts of the flesh, its lusts of the eyes and the pride of life. I am committed to studying the Word of God like never before.

7. Under the covering of the Superior Blood of Jesus Christ, I am committing large portions of the Bible to memory that I may use it both as a shield of faith and the sword of the spirit.
8. Under the covering of the Superior Blood of Jesus Christ, I am committed to enforcing the victory of Jesus on earth and in every place I go. I am committed to a life of excellence and high standards.
9. Under the covering of the Superior Blood of Jesus Christ, I am committed to winning souls. I am a fisher of men. I will henceforth be committed to attend Prayer Meetings and Bible Teaching services of the church.
10. Under the covering of the Superior Blood of Jesus Christ, I hereby make a new and resolute commitment to giving generously to the Lord, His course, and to the Storehouse (the church) from which I feed spiritually.
    I make this commitment from which I will not slack again.
11. Under the covering of the Superior Blood of Jesus Christ, I commit myself to the Lord as my refuge during times of hardship.
12. Under the covering of the Superior Blood of Jesus Christ, unto you oh Lord have I committed my course and thank you for executing judgment for me.

DAY 2
The False Pursuit of God

Yet they seek me daily, and delight to know my ways, as a nation that did righteousness, and forsook not the ordinance of their God: they ask of me the ordinances of justice; they take delight in approaching to God.
Isaiah 58:2

DAY 2: The False Pursuit of God

Today is the 2nd day of our fasting. Make amends with people you have hurt and those who have hurt you. Pray for those who despise you, persecute, and seek your harm. Forgive your offenders and enter the throne room of God with a heart that is pure and blameless.

LOG-ON: DAY 2 – Morning Prayers

Acknowledge the LORD with praise and worship. Rejoice in His loving-kindness and goodness toward you. Pray according to these prayer points for at least five minutes:

1. Under the covering of the Superior Blood of Jesus Christ, O God, make me worthy of Your calling, in the name of Jesus.
2. Under the covering of the Superior Blood of Jesus Christ, O God, deliver me from the darkness of my own mind, in the name of Jesus.
3. Under the covering of the Superior Blood of Jesus Christ, let the power of wickedness die in my heart, in the name of Jesus.
4. Under the covering of the Superior Blood of Jesus Christ, deliver me, O Lord, from the daily snares of darkness, in the name of Jesus.
5. Under the covering of the Superior Blood of Jesus Christ, O Lord, let Your watchful eye ever be upon me for my defense, in the name of Jesus.
6. Under the covering of the Superior Blood of Jesus Christ, deliver me, O Lord, from the painful evils to which I have exposed myself, in the name of Jesus.
7. Under the covering of the Superior Blood of Jesus Christ, Father, let me have unrestrained fellowship with the Lord Jesus Christ, in the name of Jesus.

8. Under the covering of the Superior Blood of Jesus Christ, increase my love for You, O God, in the name of Jesus.
9. Under the covering of the Superior Blood of Jesus Christ, O Lord, purify my heart and remove far from me iniquity and the spirit of retaliation, in the name of Jesus.
10. Under the covering of the Superior Blood of Jesus Christ, I defy my adversary by the power in the blood of Jesus.

DAY 2
The False Pursuit of God

Yet they seek me daily, and delight to know my ways, as a nation that did righteousness, and forsook not the ordinance of their God: they ask of me the ordinances of justice; they take delight in approaching to God.
Isaiah 58:2

WE NOTE FROM THE FIRST VERSE that Yahweh is displeased with His people, and He declares them rebels and barefaced sinners. Now He continues with the indictments of the crimes committed, "they seek me daily, and delight to know my ways" (v.2a); a phrase that makes them sound as if they are the epitome of faithfulness. Oftentimes, those who are deeply trenched in sin are the greatest of worshipers. They worship hard and faithfully, distraught by emotions and uncontrollable tears, yet they are an affront to Yahweh. The reason Yahweh frowns at them is not because their tears are fake; though it may be sincere, but because the heart is not fixed on change.

How many times have they run to Yahweh's altar, sobbing with unrestrained emotions, yet go back wallowing in their sins? No change occurred after that persuasive drama before His presence.

There are those, who in the heat of the moment, and in the atmosphere of worship, throw themselves to Yahweh, crying in surrender and submissiveness, yet exit the church doors with the same attitude they entered.

Dear friend, we ought to ponder on our relationship with Yahweh. Can our repentance be taken seriously by Him? Do we surrender and *un-surrender*? Have we forgotten that that which is presented to the altar is dead? So then, if we go before the altar, we must return as new creatures, and not as the same unforgiven and bitter hearted individuals.

Our pursuit of Yahweh, must be sincere and intentional. We must approach Him with the full commitment and desire to relinquish our ways, no matter how painful it maybe for us. We must trust Him with our hurts, brokenness, and heartaches.

Sometimes, an individual may be bleeding internally, with no external symptoms. Their praise and their worship may look glorious on the outside, but within, their soul is dead. If you find yourself on this path to self-destruction, let your relationship with Yahweh be deliberate. Make daily confessions, repent daily, believe in the absolute finished work of Christ in your life, and exercise faith in Him.

What's more, we must note that Yahweh is not interested in our empty promises, sensationalism and baked emotions. He is quick to detect the superficial inconsistencies in our worship:

> *"...as a nation that did righteousness, and forsook not the ordinance of their God..." (v.2b)*

It is easy to act righteous than to be righteous. To Yahweh, His people have failed the righteousness test, and forsaken His laws. This will come as a surprise to these people. They think that they have been faithful. They think that their fasting and sabbath-keeping have pleased God. What they are about to learn is that God considers them to have been majoring in minors – to have been faithfully keeping the lesser parts of the law while neglecting (in Jesus's words to the Pharisees and scribes) *"the weightier matters of the law: justice, mercy, and faith"* (Matthew 23:23). Yes fasting is important, but it is also important for us to observe the lesser requirements "and not to have left the other undone" (Matthew 23:23).

We cannot have intimacy with Yahweh if our intentions are not aligned with Him. How can we walk with Him, if we are not willing to follow His word? Amos the Prophet was sent by Yahweh to prosecute the people for a false relationship with Him; a relationship based on lies: *"Can two walk together, except they be agreed?"* (Amos 3:3). Yahweh will not have fellowship with us, unless we agree to His terms and conditions.

Our pursuit of Yahweh must be in accordance with His Word. If we do not honor His Word, then we have no fellowship with Him: *"...they ask of me righteous judgments; they delight to draw near to God"* (v.2c). The irony is that these unrighteous people are asking Yahweh for "righteous judgment." They will pray, "God, take care of those people who have hurt me so badly." They fail to understand that, if Yahweh were to render "righteous judgments," He would condemn rather than vindicate them. We must take caution, when praying for Yahweh to judge our enemies. Our own hearts must first of all be righteous.

The majority of believers today who think themselves righteous are simply self-righteous. We may declare ourselves righteous, even when Yahweh thinks otherwise of us. It is easy to call Yahweh your friend, but it is not an easy feat for Yahweh to proclaim you as His friend. You can call someone your best friend, yet they also have someone they call their best friend. How we live in righteousness is what makes us a friend of Yahweh. It was Yahweh who declared Abraham to be His friend, because he was found righteous:

> *"And the scripture was fulfilled which saith, Abraham believed God, and it was imputed unto him for righteousness: and he was called the Friend of God"* (James 2:23).

We should not assume a morally superior stance above others. We must acknowledge that our walk with Yahweh is individually different. We must help strengthen one another, and build-up each other as children of the same Kingdom.

As you go through this second day of your fasting, examine your walk with Yahweh. Are you in a false pursuit of Him?

⇒ **TIPS FOR TODAY**

Avoid Religious Appearance (Isaiah 58 verses 2)

- Avoid looking wretched, untidy, ungroomed, and pious to give others the impression that you've just arrived from the Mt. Sinai and you've had a divine encounter.

- Rather, as Jesus said, anoint yourself (put on lotion), take a good shower, brush your teeth, and keep your breath fresh for the duration of the fast. (Mathew 6:17-18).

- Be simple, be yourself, and allow the internal work of God to take place within your Spirit.

PRAYER GUIDE 2:

- Pray against the spirit of hypocrisy and deception in your heart.
- Pray for the gentle Spirit of God to come upon you throughout this entire fasting.
- Pray for purity, righteousness and holiness without self-efforts. Let the Spirit of God do the work within you and obey and give yourself to Him wholly.
- Pray against judgmental spirits, and unrighteous accusation of others.
- Pray for peace and stability of mind, and the liberty of the Holy Spirit during the fasting.

LOG-OFF: DAY 2 - Evening Prayers

Remember not the former things and the former ways, but love the LORD with all you are and bless His good name today.

Enter these prayer points (Use each prayer point to pray for at least five minutes):

1. Under the covering of the Superior Blood of Jesus Christ, plant my heart, O Lord in Your ways and create a deep hunger for you in my heart, in the name of Jesus.

2. Under the covering of the Superior Blood of Jesus Christ, Holy Ghost, show me where I have fallen and help me correct my ways, in the name of Jesus.

3. Under the covering of the Superior Blood of Jesus Christ, Jesus, remove not my candlestick from Your presence, in the name of Jesus.

4. Under the covering of the Superior Blood of Jesus Christ, Every power disgracing me before God, BE DISGRACED, in the name of Jesus.

5. Under the covering of the Superior Blood of Jesus Christ, O Lord, let no one defile me anymore, in the name of Jesus.

6. Under the covering of the Superior Blood of Jesus Christ, Lord God Almighty, visit me afresh and let Your light shine upon me once again, in the name of Jesus.

7. Under the covering of the Superior Blood of Jesus Christ, Holy Ghost, quicken me and bring me alive, in the name of Jesus.

8. Under the covering of the Superior Blood of Jesus Christ, I shall walk in the light of the Lord, in the name of Jesus.

9. Under the covering of the Superior Blood of Jesus Christ, plant in me, O Lord, the tree of life for my healing and the healing of the nations, in the name of Jesus.

10. Under the covering of the Superior Blood of Jesus Christ, O Lord, subdue in me, the love of sin, in the name of Jesus.

DAY 3
The Fasting God Despises

Wherefore have we fasted, say they, and thou seest not? wherefore have we afflicted our soul, and thou takest no knowledge? Behold, in the day of your fast ye find pleasure, and exact all your labours.
- Isaiah 58:3a

DAY 3: The Fasting God Despises

Today is the third day of our Fasting and Prayer. Allow God to use this fasting period to reshape your life and destiny. Apply yourself wholly to this fasting season. Let it be a period of consecration and sanctification for you. Make a covenant to seek the face of God in this period without compromising yourself in any way that is displeasing to God.

LOG-ON: DAY 3 – Morning Prayers

Enter these prayer points (Use each prayer point to pray for at least five minutes):

1. Under the covering of the Superior Blood of Jesus Christ, empower me to live as You would have me to, in the name of Jesus.
2. Under the covering of the Superior Blood of Jesus Christ, empower me, O Lord, to walk in love and a spirit of forgiveness, in the name of Jesus.
3. Under the covering of the Superior Blood of Jesus Christ, O Lord, let me not be at my own disposal, in the name of Jesus.
4. Under the covering of the Superior Blood of Jesus Christ, my name will not be a reproach and an embarrassment to the kingdom of God, in the name of Jesus.
5. Under the covering of the Superior Blood of Jesus Christ, Father, come with your mighty power and expel every rebellious spirit in me, in the name of Jesus.
6. Under the covering of the Superior Blood of Jesus Christ, Father, come with your mighty power and reign supreme in my life, in the name of Jesus.

7. Under the covering of the Superior Blood of Jesus Christ, Father, come as a Teacher and lead me into all truth, in the name of Jesus.
8. Under the covering of the Superior Blood of Jesus Christ, Father, come as a Teacher and fill me with understanding, in the name of Jesus.
9. Under the covering of the Superior Blood of Jesus Christ, Father, come as a shield and protect me against the arrows of the enemy, in the name of Jesus.
10. Under the covering of the Superior Blood of Jesus Christ, Father, come as joy, and quench every spirit of oppression and depression in my soul, in the name of Jesus.

DAY 3
The Fasting God Despises

Wherefore have we fasted, say they, and thou seest not? wherefore have we afflicted our soul, and thou takest no knowledge? Behold, in the day of your fast ye find pleasure, and exact all your labours.
Isaiah 58:3a

THIS IS THE SINCERE COMPLAINT of many believers I have spoken to over the years of my pastoral work: "God, how come we've fasted so much, and prayed so well, and yet You haven't answered our prayers? Don't you owe us something here?" This is the complaint of the people in this verse of scripture. They fasted with the hope that they would receive something from God. We believe that if we fulfill our requirement to fast (abstain from food), then God should return the favor by conferring blessings on us.

In other words, most believers ignorantly assume that fasting establishes an obligation that God is duty-bound to meet. This is absolutely not true. God is not bound to answer our prayers because we fast. In fact, we do not fast to change God's mind or to manipulate His actions. Fasting is a spiritual act that creates room for us to spend time with God. It removes hindrances between us and God. It does away with the things that normally clog our intimacy with Him. Fasting does not place any obligatory demands on God to answer our prayers. Indeed, we fast because it emboldens our prayer life, and not because it makes God powerless against us.

The idea that God is obligated to answer these people because they fasted is a "quid pro quo" theology. We cannot do anything to manipulate the blessings of Yahweh. Even in our giving of tithes, offering or any special thing, the motive isn't to bribe God. Yahweh simply doesn't need our money but He demands our sacrifice. Hence, anything we deem important (for example our money, treasure, possessions, time, career) must be sacrificed to Him as an act of submission to His worship.

The mistake many of us make is to think of fasting as a "quid pro quo". In other words, "God, do this for me because I fasted." We must not be tempted to play these games with God. Yahweh is God, and we are His creation. Hence, Yahweh, has a right as Creator to impose obligations on us, but we have no right as the creation to impose obligations on Him. We cannot condition Him to do anything that His Word does not sanction.

We can only impress upon Yahweh to do that which is in His will to do. We can only command Him because He bids us to do so, and not because we have authority over Him:

> *Thus says the LORD, The Holy One of Israel, and his Maker: "Ask Me of things to come concerning My sons; And concerning the work of My hands, you command Me. - (Isaiah 45:11).*

We have such an audacious right, not because we are entitled to it, but because He has bestowed upon us His grace to function like Him.

> *And I will give you the keys of the kingdom of heaven, and whatever you bind on earth will be bound in heaven, and whatever you loose on earth will be loosed in heaven." (Matthew 16:19)*

If we fast and pray in accordance with His will, and not our corrupt motive, then "If ye shall ask any thing in my name, I will do *it*" (John 14:14).

As you go through this day of the fast, remember that it is not your fasting that will steer the Hand of God in your favor, but it is your heart surrendered to Him wholly during the fasting period.

⇒ **TIPS FOR TODAY:**

Follow the highway of Righteousness and Holiness (Isaiah 58 verse 3)
- Be humble and not self-seeking during the fasting.
- God is the focus of the fasting, not your issues.
- Let it be your motive to seek God first of all as your highest priority, and not your desires.

- The goal is to win God's heart to you. The appeal is not to convince God to win your heart, He already loves you, and He sacrificed for you on Calvary. It is now your turn to sacrifice to win Him into your life.
- Make this fasting about devotion and not about your grocery list.
- Your fasting is not a challenge or a competition with anyone, do not compare.
- Make a vow of consecration to God as you go through this fasting.

PRAYER GUIDE 3:

- Pray that God will create in you a clean heart.
- Pray that the fire of the Holy Spirit will purge your motives to be pure.
- Pray that the LORD will visit you and satisfy your heart.
- Pray that His love will renew your confidence in Him.
- Pray for a stronger intimacy and a lifestyle of devotion to Him.
- Pray that you will rekindle the first love you had for Him.
- Pray for His continuous guidance and strength even as you go through this fast.

LOG-OFF: DAY 3 – Evening Prayers

Enter these prayer points before you go to bed (Use each prayer point to pray for at least five minutes):

1. Under the covering of the Superior Blood of Jesus Christ, O Lord, give me grace to be transformed into Thy likeness, in the name of Jesus.
2. Under the covering of the Superior Blood of Jesus Christ, O Lord, give me grace to be consecrated wholly to You, in the name of Jesus.
3. Under the covering of the Superior Blood of Jesus Christ, O Lord, give me grace to overcome my weaknesses, in the name of Jesus.
4. Under the covering of the Superior Blood of Jesus Christ, O Lord, deliver me from attachments to unclean things, in the name of Jesus.
5. Under the covering of the Superior Blood of Jesus Christ, O Lord, deliver me from attachments to the wrong associations, in the name of Jesus.
6. Under the covering of the Superior Blood of Jesus Christ, O Lord, deliver me from attachments to evil passions, in the name of Jesus.
7. Under the covering of the Superior Blood of Jesus Christ, O Lord, deliver me from impure thoughts and wicked imaginations, in the name of Jesus.
8. Under the covering of the Superior Blood of Jesus Christ, O God, arise and open to me the springs of divine knowledge, in the name of Jesus.
9. Under the covering of the Superior Blood of Jesus Christ, let my life be a testimony of your glory, in the name of Jesus.
10. Under the covering of the Superior Blood of Jesus Christ, O Lord, fight for me and let my foes flee, in the name of Jesus.

DAY 4
Fasting Without God

Behold, in the day of your fast ye find pleasure, and exact all your labours (Isaiah 58:3b).

DAY 4: Fasting Without God

This is day four of our fasting. As you go through this day, be mindful of your activity. Remember that a fast means denying yourself of what you want so you can give God that which is required. Take caution not to spend time doing unnecessary things when that time can be dedicated to prayer. Find time to pray, rest, meditate on God's Word, and practice listening to His voice.

Ask yourself what does God want me to do for someone today? During fasting, we deny ourselves of something we love, so that we can let someone have it. Today, go and do something for someone you would love done for you. Bless someone with what you have denied yourself of.

LOG-ON: DAY 4 – Morning Prayers

Pray today for an increase in your personal faith. Ask God to show you that which you believe is impossible, and then specifically ask Him to give you the faith to trust Him to make it possible. Ask God to give you a refreshing measure of faith to believe that with Him all things are possible.

Make these confessions to establish your identity in Christ Jesus. Spend 3 to 10 minutes on each prayer point:

1. Under the covering of the Superior Blood of Jesus Christ, I am not what the world thinks or says I am.
2. Under the covering of the Superior Blood of Jesus Christ, I am not what the devil or the kingdom of darkness says, imagines or has designed me to be.

3. Under the covering of the Superior Blood of Jesus Christ, I am not the picture of what my idolatrous forefathers wished I should be.
4. Under the covering of the Superior Blood of Jesus Christ, I am not what the unregenerate mind of any friend thinks I am.
5. Under the covering of the Superior of the Superior Blood of Jesus Christ, I am not what my father and mother think or want me to be.
6. Under the covering of the Superior Blood of Jesus Christ, I am not what my village wickedness, household wickedness and environmental wickedness want me to be.
7. Under the covering of the Superior Blood of Jesus Christ, I am not a picture of what the national economy and institutionalized wickedness have restructured the people to be.
8. Under the covering of the Blood of Jesus Christ, I am not what I think I am.
9. Under the covering of the Superior Blood of Jesus Christ, I am who the Word of God says I am.
10. Under the covering of the Superior Blood of Jesus Christ, I am an express image of Jehovah God on earth.

DAY 4

The Fast Without God

Behold, in the day of your fast ye find pleasure, and exact all your labours (Isaiah 58:3b)

THE PEOPLE IN DEFIANCE of Yahweh were saying, "God we did this for you, why haven't you done this for us?" They were disappointed that Yahweh ignored their fasting. In response, Yahweh states His case against them. Their fasting is profusely flawed. They have not fasted to honor Yahweh but for their own selfish gain. They have assumed Yahweh will reward their fasting, so they fasted to earn the reward. Their mistake was that they had no intention to give devotion to Yahweh, but to gain a blessing from Him. Their fasting, therefore, was exactly the opposite of sincere fasting.

The fasting Yahweh demands, is an act of self-denial. Instead, they offered him a self-centered hunger strike for a reward. Their fasting was not an act of humility but of pride.

There is no virtue in that kind of selfishness, and they should not have expected a reward.

We must all examine the motive of our fasting. It is imperative to extricate our selfish interests in our pursuit of Yahweh. We must first of all win God's heart and in so doing, He will take care of our needs out of love:

> *And it shall come to pass, that before they call, I will answer; and while they are yet speaking, I will hear. Isaiah 65:24*

When we fast without Yahweh at the center, we will gain nothing but weight loss. During the fasting, we must be give our full attention to Him alone. We must be careful how we engage in unnecessary activities and leisure that could instead be our prayer time and moments shared with Yahweh.

The fundamental problem in most of our fasting is pointed out by Yahweh: "...in the day of your fast you...exact all your labours" (v.3c). This deserves emphasis. Many have oppressed their neighbors whilst even in a state of fasting. Most of us continue to express such cruel behavior toward others even as we claim to be fasting. It is my prayer that you will not find yourself in this disposition. This will be a season of refreshing for you. Yahweh will hear your voice in this fasting period, and you will experience His visitation:

> *Behold, I will send my messenger, and he shall prepare the way before me: and the Lord, whom ye seek, shall suddenly come to his temple, even the messenger of the covenant, whom ye delight in: behold, he shall come, saith the LORD of hosts. (Malachi 3:1)*

If we believe, we will experience Him. Keep alert as you pray during this fasting and keep staring at the door for that visitation: *"For surely there is an end; and thine expectation shall not be cut off"* *(Proverbs 23:18).*

⇒ TIPS FOR TODAY

God demands to be the center of your Fasting (Isaiah 58 verse 3b,c)

- Compose yourself during the period of the fast.
- Avoid exacting all your pleasures: such as sitting by the TV or movies all day. If possible, only watch necessary programs such as the News during the fasting period. Use all other entertainment or leisure time to pray and to read the Bible.
- Make time for the LORD; don't be given to many extracurricular activities. Come home early after work or school, or any other duty and give yourself and the rest of the day entirely to God.
- Don't work double time or overtime. Close from your duties regularly and make sacrificial time for the LORD.
- Avoid contentions and strife with anyone; relative or friend during this fasting period.
- Make amends with people who you normally have a problem with, and extend a hand of sincere love and godly conduct.
- Do not fast "against" anyone: Do not fast to kill, to destroy, or to harm anyone. God is not interested in your revenge or oppression of others.

PRAYER GUIDE 4:
- Pray for the power of self-control and discipline.
- Pray for divine enablement to spend more intimate time with the LORD for your spiritual maturity.
- Pray that the Holy Spirit will feed you with the Word of God daily as you read.
- Pray and remember the names of people you have offended, or grieved, and repent. Ask the LORD for the heart to forgive those who have offended or grieved you.
- Pray for those who are in contention with you that God will restore peace and stability in those relationships.
- Pray for any relative, (for example mother, father, or sibling) with whom you are not on speaking terms. Ask the LORD to give you a heart of reconciliation and the sweetness of the Spirit of forgiveness. Pray for spiritual healing within your family.
- Pray for a heart of love and righteous judgment toward everyone.

LOG-OFF: DAY 4 – Evening Prayers

Confessions: Make these confessions to establish your identity in Christ Jesus. Pray each of these prayer points for 3 to 10 minutes as necessary:

1. Under the covering of the Superior Blood of Jesus Christ, the Bible says because I believe and receive Jesus Christ, power has been given to me to become a son of God, and I am empowered to trample upon serpents and scorpions and all the powers of the enemy.

2. Under the covering of the Superior Blood of Jesus Christ, I am empowered to use the name of Jesus to cast out demons and heal the sick.

3. Under the covering of the Superior Blood of Jesus Christ, I am empowered to bind, to loose and to decree things, and the Bible says wherever my voice is heard no one can ask me why.

4. Under the covering of the Superior Blood of Jesus Christ, I confess, my voice is the voice of a king that is full of authority.

5. Under the covering of the Superior Blood of Jesus Christ, I am commanded and empowered by my God to subdue and to exercise dominion. For I am made a little lower than the angels and God has crowned me with glory and honor, and has also made me to have dominion over all the works of His hands.

6. Under the covering of the Superior Blood of Jesus Christ, the devil that was against my authority as God's representative on earth has been destroyed by Christ. Once again, the keys of the kingdom of heaven are given to me and because I am a member

of the body of Christ, which is the Church, the gates of hell cannot prevail against me.

7. Under the covering of the Superior Blood of Jesus Christ, because the grace of God is upon my life as the light of His glory, I am full of divine favor. I am a partaker of all of heaven's spiritual blessings.

8. Under the covering of the Superior Blood of Jesus, I boldly declare, I am an overcomer. The Bible says whosoever is born of God overcomes the world, and this is the victory that overcomes the world, even my faith.

9. Under the covering of the Superior Blood of Jesus Christ, I declare, in faith I overcome ungodly worry, anxiety, heaviness of spirit, sorrow, depression, lust of the eyes, and lust of the flesh.

10. Under the covering of the Superior Blood of Jesus Christ, I declare, in faith I have overcome all the tricks of the devil, for it is written, greater is Jesus Christ who dwells in me than the devil that is in the world.

DAY 5
The Tongue In Fasting

Behold, ye fast for strife and debate, and to smite with the fist of wickedness: ye shall not fast as ye do this day, to make your voice to be heard on high. – Isaiah 58:4

DAY 5: The Tongue In Fasting

We now enter day five of this fasting. The tongue can be an instrument of great peace, great inspiration or of great destruction and devastation, on the world stage or in your life. That's why you must learn to master your tongue. How many times have you said things and regretted it? How many times have you spoken out and wished you could take the words back? So many people I know, have so many regrets about what they have said.

Master your tongue or it will master your life, ruin your reputation, and destroy your relationships. If you want to master your tongue, you can read nothing better than the passage in James 3:12.

LOG-ON: DAY 5 – Morning Prayers

Make these confessions to begin the day. Stand on each of these prayer points for at least five minutes as necessary:

1. Under the covering of the Superior Blood of Jesus Christ, I tread down all temptations by the power in the blood of Jesus.
2. Under the covering of the Superior Blood of Jesus Christ, I resist the scheming of darkness by the power in the blood of Jesus.
3. Under the covering of the Superior Blood of Jesus Christ, I renounce and denounce any evil gifts designed to entice me from God and Church, by the power in the blood of Jesus.
4. Under the covering of the Superior Blood of Jesus Christ, O Lord, make my walk with You deeper, in

the name of Jesus. I refuse to be a shallow and powerless Christian.
5. Under the covering of the Superior Blood of Jesus Christ, I shall not walk daily with evildoers, gossipers, liars, and backbiters, in the name of Jesus.
6. Under the covering of the Superior Blood of Jesus Christ, empower me, O Lord, to walk by Your side, in the name of Jesus.
7. Under the covering of the Superior Blood of Jesus Christ, empower me, O Lord, to listen to Your voice, in the name of Jesus.
8. Under the covering of the Superior Blood of Jesus Christ, empower me, O Lord, to be clothed with Your grace, in the name of Jesus.
9. Under the covering of the Superior Blood of Jesus Christ, empower me, O Lord, to be adorned with Thy righteousness, in the name of Jesus.
10. Under the covering of the Superior Blood of Jesus Christ, let me, O Lord, study and stand for discipleship, in the name of Jesus.

DAY 5
The Tongue In Fasting

Behold, ye fast for strife and debate, and to smite with the fist of wickedness: ye shall not fast as ye do this day, to make your voice to be heard on high. – Isaiah 58:4

WHILE IT SEEMS HARD TO IMAGINE that an act of devotion would lead to violence, I read a news story about two men who got into an argument about which of them knew the Bible better. They argued for a time, and then one of them went away and came back armed with a gun. He shot and killed the other man. True story!

Furthermore, consider the heated discussions of abortion or homosexuality or other hot-button issues at our denominational conferences. Is it beyond imagining that such discussions could lead to violence? All around us, there are heated Christian debates on doctrines and theology that has embittered many and destroyed several lives.

What good is our fasting when we go on fighting and quarreling. It is amazing the number of Christians who go through a month of fasting, and yet are in quarreling with their mother, father, sibling or a friend. How can you go into a fast, and continue it to the end without reconciling with those you have a grudge against or those who you haven't forgiven?

Jesus made a remarkable analysis of what true genuine prayer before God means:

> *So if you are about to place your gift on the altar and remember that someone is angry with you, leave your gift there in front of the altar. Make peace with that person, then come back and offer your gift to God. – Matthew 5:23-24*

In like manner, when we are fasting, we are praying. As a result, we cannot keep strife in our hearts and believe that Yahweh will reward us.

Moreover, remember that true godliness affects your relationships. There people were doing something that was supposed to affect their relationship with God. But something that affects your relationship with God ought to also affect your relationship with others.

God will not honor a fasting that is flawed: *"you don't fast this day so as to make your voice to be heard on high"* (v. 4b).

When we fast, the tongue must bless Yahweh, and not be used to curse others. We must have command of the tongue. It must be tamed under the subjection of our desire to please God.

⇒ TIPS FOR TODAY

The Tongue must be consecrated to God (Isaiah 58 verse 4)

- Beware, the words your tongue produces can destroy your entire family. Truly death and life are in the tongue.
- Our tongue can be a guard protecting our integrity, or it can reveal the evil inside our hearts. So what about your tongue? Does it produce peace or reveal hypocrisy?
- If you can master your tongue you can master your whole body.
- Tie your tongue, and avoid gossip during your fasting period.
- Avoid that destructive spirit called innuendo. It is like gossip in that it spreads destruction. It also insinuates something and leaves the listener to draw their own conclusions. It goes like this: "I saw the two of them together, and they did seem very close. Now I'm not saying there's anything in it, but…"
- Our words have power, and they last. You cannot just say things. You cannot just blurt them out and then walk away as if nothing has happened. What we say can't be retracted easily. That's why I suggest that you should be slow to speak. Think through what you are about to say instead of exploding in anger!

PRAYER GUIDE 5:
- Pray for everyone who has offended you.
- Pray for your enemies; those who persecute you, tell lies, or gossip about you.
- Mention the name of the persons you do not like and pray diligently that God will bless them, just as you would pray for yourself.
- If there's anyone in your life who brings you misery and pain, it's time to pray for them.
- Pray for your marriage, your relationships with friends, and your loved ones.
- Pray for the unity in your local church and the universal church.
- Pray that Yahweh takes control of your tongue, and that the Holy Spirit will speak through your mouth during this fasting period.

LOG-ON: DAY 5 – Evening Prayers

Make these confessions to conclude the day in prayer. Stand on each of these prayer points for at least five minutes as necessary:

1. Under the covering of the Superior Blood of Jesus Christ, O Lord, renovate my life for Your use, in the name of Jesus.
2. Under the covering of the Superior Blood of Jesus Christ, O Lord, remove pride from my life in the name of Jesus.
3. Under the covering of the Superior Blood of Jesus Christ, O Lord, implant in me true lowliness of spirit, in the name of Jesus.
4. Under the covering of the Superior Blood of Jesus Christ, O Lord, break me, then mold me up, in the name of Jesus.
5. Under the covering of the Superior Blood of Jesus Christ, O Lord, mortify me to this world, in the name of Jesus.
6. Under the covering of the Superior Blood of Jesus Christ, O Lord, secure me in your grace, in the name of Jesus.
7. Under the covering of the Superior Blood of Jesus Christ, O Lord, destroy in me, every clinging tendency toward self-righteousness, in the name of Jesus.
8. Under the covering of the Superior Blood of Jesus Christ, let my life reflect Jesus.
9. Under the covering of the Superior Blood of Jesus Christ, the Lord will uphold me in spirit and truth.
10. Under the covering of the Superior Blood of Jesus Christ, everything I lay my hands on will result in prosperity.

DAY 6

The Rejected Fast

Is it such a fast that I have chosen? a day for a man to afflict his soul? is it to bow down his head as a bulrush, and to spread sackcloth and ashes under him? wilt thou call this a fast, and an acceptable day to the LORD? - Isaiah 58:5

DAY 6: The Rejected Fast

We now enter day six of our fasting as we continue our consecration for God's renovation in our lives. Not all fasting is acceptable to God. As we go through this day, may we seek to please Him, and do what will honor and invite Him into our lives.

LOG-ON: DAY 6 – Morning Prayers

Make these confessions to begin the day. Stand on each of these prayer points for at least five minutes as necessary:

1. Under the covering of the Superior Blood of Jesus Christ, we confess our sins and ask for forgiveness. I forgive those who have sinned against me from the past through to this moment, and will continue to do so.

2. Under the covering of the Blood of Jesus Christ, I plead the Blood of Jesus over any sins committed by my parents and ancestors. I cancel through the Blood, any satanic covenants, agreements, exchanges, vows or transactions made over our lives, bodies, souls and circumstances.

3. Under the covering of the Blood of Jesus Christ, I declare that we are redeemed from the hand of the devil by the Blood of Jesus. I declare that all satanic thrones, altars, dominions, principalities, powers, rulers of darkness, spiritual hosts of wickedness, and all satanic works have no power or authority over us. I declare that satanic harassment and intimidation have no effect on us.

4. Under the covering of the Blood of Jesus Christ, I command that every planting of the enemy shall be pulled out of our lives and the lives of our loved ones. I arrest all satanic projections, fiery darts, arrows, witchcraft activities and evil prayers.

5. Under the covering of the Blood of Jesus Christ, I declare that the enemy is permanently denied access into our lives and destinies. I take and maintain our position of being seated in Jesus in heavenly places and the devil is under our feet. I walk in dominion, power, and God's prophetic purpose - NOW!

6. Under the covering of the Blood of Jesus Christ, I declare that what was written of us in the volume of the books, as well as our prophetic destinies and purposes, will be fulfilled now without delay or interference. I declare that divine timing, strategic relationships, open doors and favor in high places shall manifest continually in our lives.

7. Under the covering of the Blood of Jesus Christ, I command divine solutions for every problem in our lives to manifest. I command every satanic mystery, cycle and mechanism to be permanently exposed, decoded and destroyed through the Blood of Jesus.

8. Under the covering of the Blood of Jesus Christ, I declare that every legality, technicality, ordinance and judgment issued against us in the realms of the spirit be overturned. I command an injunction and restraining order be issued and enforced against all acts of injustice and harassment (Colossians 2:14).

9. Under the covering of the Blood of Jesus Christ, I declare that God will rule in our favor and the

divine order for our restoration and restitution shall be signed with the Blood of the Lamb and enforced by the angels of God on every level. Our victory shall be published throughout heaven, on earth and underneath the earth. All shame and reproach shall be washed away and we will receive double honor.

10. Under the covering of the Blood of Jesus Christ, I declare that we have overcome the enemy by the Blood of the Lamb and the word of our testimony - Jesus saved us from the laws of sin and death. I activate the Blood of Jesus to speak innocence for us, to silence every accusation whether it is true or false, to locate, arrest and bind every power operating behind the scenes (Revelation 12:11).

DAY 6

The Rejected Fast

Is it such a fast that I have chosen? a day for a man to afflict his soul? is it to bow down his head as a bulrush, and to spread sackcloth and ashes under him? wilt thou call this a fast, and an acceptable day to the LORD?
- Isaiah 58:5

FASTING CAN BE ABUSED to create a false sense of spirituality. This warning about "false spirituality" is part of what Jesus was dealing with in His concerns over fasting:

> *Moreover when ye fast, be not, as the hypocrites, of a sad countenance: for they disfigure their faces, that they may appear unto men to fast. Verily I say unto you, They have their reward. But thou, when thou fastest, anoint thine head, and wash thy face; That*

> *thou appear not unto men to fast, but unto thy Father which is in secret: and thy Father, which seeth in secret, shall reward thee openly.*
> *(Mat 6:16-18 KJV)*

Fasting can actually "backfire" on you. You may start off wanting to fast for the right reasons, and end up further away from the Lord because of your own spiritual pride.

Yahweh in Isaiah 58 verse 5, asks if they think that He desires their self-serving actions. Do they imagine that it is an act of humility to manipulate God? Do they believe that their external observances (bowing the head and dressing in sackcloth and ashes) please God? This verse doesn't go so far as to say that these actions are unacceptable to God, but God's questions clearly presuppose a "No!" answer.

We observe that it is possible to display a sense of spirituality that on the outside looks very much impressive. We may pray eloquently, know our Bible quotations, even lead worship or serve in the church, but they can all be done for the wrong reasons.

There is a fast that Yahweh utterly rejects. Not all fasting is acceptable to Him. This is why some of us fast and receive nothing; because we fast amiss.

Yahweh asks a question, "Is it such a fast that I have chosen?" In understanding the Law of the Fast, we first note that, the fast is chosen by God. In other words, God requires us to fast. Hence, He appointed and chose a fast for us. Secondly, we do not determine the rules of the fast. The designator of the fast is also the determinator of the fast. If we fast, we must do it God's way. If not, it is flawed and unacceptable.

God expects our fasting to extend beyond the abstinence of food into godly acts of touching others through our fast.

⇒ TIPS FOR TODAY

The Tongue Must Be Consecrated to God (Isaiah 58 verse 5).

- Fasting is not just about not eating. We must make time for prayer.
- Strategically develop the love for "activity prayers". In other words, pray during your daily routine activities. For example, pray when in the shower, when vacuuming, when driving, when cooking, when at home on your computer, when doing your laundry or cleaning the house. We can find time to pray, if we desire to pray.
- At work, you can tithe ten percent of your lunch break to pray or read the Bible.
- Pray for perhaps 30 seconds when you take that bathroom break.
- Be careful not to spend your work hours praying. Unless, you take a vacation to fast, God expects you to be working, so wisely divide your time accordingly.
- Keep yourself descent and well-groomed. No one should smell your breath or have reason to believe that you have not showered all day. Put the sackcloth and ashes on your heart and not on your body.

PRAYER GUIDE 6:
- Pray for your family. Is there anyone who isn't saved in the family?
- Pray for your friends. Is there any amongst them who isn't saved?
- Pray for people you meet on your way to work or in the supermarket.
- Pray for the love of God in your life for others.
- Pray for the gift of discernment in your spiritual walk.
- Pray for the power to dream with clarity.
- Pray that Yahweh will be a gatekeeper for your family.

LOG-OFF: DAY 6 – Evening Prayers

Make these confessions to establish your identity in Christ Jesus. Spend at least five minutes on each prayer point:

1. Under the covering of the Superior Blood of Jesus Christ, I am fashioned after the likeness of the Creator of heaven and earth.
2. Under the covering of the Superior Blood of Jesus Christ, I am regenerated by the blood of Jesus.
3. Under the covering of the Superior Blood of Jesus Christ, I am ransomed from the powers of death and hell.
4. Under the covering of the Superior Blood of Jesus Christ, I am blood washed.
5. Under the covering of the Superior Blood of Jesus Christ, I boldly declare, I am redeemed.
6. Under the covering of the Superior Blood of Jesus Christ, I boldly declare, I am justified by Christ.
7. Under the covering of the Superior Blood of Jesus Christ, I boldly declare, I am made to be the righteousness of God through Christ.
8. Under the covering of the Superior Blood of Jesus Christ, I boldly declare, I am a believer of the Word of Truth.
9. Under the covering of the Superior Blood of Jesus Christ, I boldly confess, I am born again.
10. Under the covering of the Superior Blood of Jesus Christ, I boldly announce, I am heaven-bound; my citizenship is in heaven.

DAY 7
Breaking the Chains of Wickedness

Is not this the fast that I have chosen? to loose the bands of wickedness, to undo the heavy burdens, and to let the oppressed go free, and that ye break every yoke?
– Isaiah 58:6

DAY 7: Breaking the Chains of Wickedness

It is easy to go without food for a day or to dress in humble attire, especially if we think that we will receive a blessing from God for doing so. It is much more difficult to readily do what pleases God; to forgive those who have caused us much pain; to break yokes that bind people to darkness.

LOG-ON: DAY 7 – Morning Prayers

Make these confessions to establish your identity in Christ Jesus. Spend at least five minutes on each prayer point:

1. Under the covering of the Superior Blood of Jesus Christ, I boldly declare, I am seated with Christ in heavenly places far above principalities and powers.

2. Under the covering of the Superior Blood of Jesus Christ, I boldly declare, I am a priest and a king (Queen) ordained by Christ to rule here on earth.

3. Under the covering of the Superior Blood of Jesus Christ, I boldly proclaim, I am the fear and the dread of God against the kingdom of darkness.

4. Under the covering of the Superior Blood of Jesus Christ, I boldly confess, I am a dwelling place of the Holy Spirit of God.

5. Under the covering of the Superior Blood of Jesus Christ, I am built up together and attached with other children of God into a holy habitation of God. The Word of God says, I am a royal priesthood, I am a holy nation, I am a chosen generation, and a peculiar person to the nation.

6. Under the covering of the Superior Blood of Jesus Christ, I boldly confess, I am special in the sight of God.

7. Under the covering of the Superior Blood of Jesus Christ, I boldy confess and declare, this year is my year of the great commission – I will do God's will.

8. Under the covering of the Blood of Jesus Christ, in the name of Jesus, I command every strongman operating in our lives to be stripped of their authority and assignments concerning us and our families. I declare that they are bound and all of their weapons are destroyed. I command that the ground troops of Satan, persons without bodies and human vessels be captured, stripped of their power, desensitized and permanently disorganized.

9. Under the covering of the Blood of Jesus Christ, I overthrow the wisdom tables of the wicked and scatter them wherever and whenever they gather. I release weapons of mass destruction upon their headquarters and destroy all their weapons and means of retaliation. I advance, take and rule their territory by the power of the Holy Ghost and in the name of our LORD Jesus.

10. Under the covering of the Blood of Jesus Christ, I command the destruction and removal of every form of witchcraft, sorcery and divination in our lives and the life of the church. I command the arrest and removal of every Jezebel spirit and the spirits of rebellion, immorality and subversion operating in our lives and the life of the church.

DAY 7

Breaking the Chains of Wickedness

Is not this the fast that I have chosen? to loose the bands of wickedness, to undo the heavy burdens, and to let the oppressed go free, and that ye break every yoke? – Isaiah 58:6

YOUR CONSECRATION FROM DAY ONE has empowered you to break the bonds of wickedness and every heavy yoke of limitation. In this verse of scripture (Isaiah 58:6), Yahweh introduces us to the kind of fasting that He likes; the fast prescribed by Him.

We discover that fasting Yahweh's way, is to first, *"loose the bond of wickedness"* (Isaiah 58:6a, NKJV)

The word picture given here is really powerful. A bond (Hebrew: *chartsubbah*) is something you would use to bind someone so that they lose their freedom. Some physical bonds would be chains or ropes. Yet Yahweh is not speaking simply of physical bondages. Yahweh is speaking of spiritual bondages. We are to fast to loose the bonds of wickedness. There are people who are literally enslaved and in spiritual bondage today. May I remind you that there are some in your family in bondage to the vices of the spirit of darkness, and God is alerting you in this fasting season to target your prayers toward their deliverance? Yes, this is a charge of the divine agenda for fasting. When we fast, God gives us power to exercise deliverance on a wider and higher scale.

I believe that whom the Son sets free is free indeed. God wants us to be free (John 8:36). If you are a believer in Jesus there should be nothing in your life that exerts power over you. You should not be addicted to anything. Yet perhaps there are things in your life that you would like to lay down but have been unable to:

- ✓ You say, "I've tried to quit smoking, but I can't!" I say, try fasting!

- ✓ You say, "I don't want to do drugs anymore." But I just struggle. I say, try fasting!

- ✓ You say, "I don't want to watch porn anymore." And I say, try fasting!

- ✓ You say, "I just can't seem to stop cussing." I say, try fasting! Again.

- ✓ You say, "I keep on getting drunk and I want to be free." I say, try fasting!

- ✓ You "I don't know how to control my temper." I say, try fasting! Again, and again.

These are some of things that the Bible calls bondages. Satan wants to keep people bound up in sin. But we can fast and we can pray, and God will answer and He can set people free. God has ordained that when we get serious about walking in victory, we would demonstrate it through fasting.

Some of you are thinking, well how does that work exactly? When we fast for our own selves, we are enacting a Biblical principle. There is a principle in the Word that talks about crucifying the flesh. The flesh is that part of us or others that desire to satisfy or gratify the sinful nature. Every time you say no to eating, you are crucifying the flesh. Every time you say no to dinner and go to pray, you are building up your spirit man and you are decreasing the power that the flesh has over you. So, it stands to reason that if you can control your appetite for food, you can control it for any other fleshly desire.

Besides that, when you fast, you are drawing near to God. And when you get near to him, He gets near to you. He will help you.

When you are fasting for others to be delivered from addiction God sees that, and He is able to turn up the heat of His Holy Spirit power. God is able to bring conviction by the power of the Holy Spirit. God is able to wake up the people you are fasting for, in the night. God is able to bring people you don't even know into their lives. Fasting and prayer work.

⇒ **TIPS FOR TODAY**
1. **Break every yoke of limitation and every curse imputed over your bloodline.**
   - Pray for all your family members and friends that they'll find peace and liberty through the saving power of Jesus Christ.

2. **This day acknowledge that your light has broken forth. (vv.8)**
   - Let your star begin to shine after today.
   - Pray and make prophetic declarations over your health.
   - Let the glory of the LORD be seen over your life.

PRAYER GUIDE 7:
   - Pray breaking every yoke of bondage in your bloodline.
   - Pray removing every burden in your bloodline: mention those burdens by name if you know them.
   - Pray against family limitations such as genetic diseases in your family and age limitation in the bloodline.
   - Pray against any spirit of stagnancy and demotion within your bloodline.
   - Pray against the spirit of bareness in your bloodline.
   - Pray against the yoke of marital separation in your family or bloodline.
   - Pray against any inherited curses or problems within your bloodline.
   - Pray against iniquities upon your bloodline.
   - Pray for the breaking forth of your light.
   - Pray that your star will shine in this season.
   - Pray for healing and recovering.

LOG-OFF: DAY 7 – Evening Prayers

Stand on these prayer points for at least five minutes and pray:

1. Thank the LORD for your family.
2. Confirm your faith and salvation in the name of Jesus.
3. Under the covering of the Blood of Jesus Christ, I saturate my entire family and bloodline in the superior blood of Jesus Christ.
4. Under the covering of the Blood of Jesus Christ, I decree the consuming fire of the Holy Spirit to run through my bloodline and cleanse us of any iniquities now in Jesus' name.
5. Under the covering of the Superior Blood of Jesus Christ, I commit my (mention name of person) before the LORD and evict any form of addiction (name it) in your life right now by the Blood of Jesus.
6. Under the covering of the Superior Blood of Jesus Christ, You spirit of (name it) addiction ruling in the life of (name the person), your contract has expired, perish now by fire in Jesus' name.
7. Under the covering of the Superior Blood of Jesus Christ, I ask for the redemptive power of the superior blood of Jesus to cover any teenager magnetized by the demons and addiction of my father's bloodline.
8. Under the covering of the Superior Blood of Jesus Christ, I deploy the redemptive power of the blood of Jesus to cover any teenager magnetized by any demons and addictions projecting from my mother's bloodline.
9. Under the covering of the Superior Blood of Jesus Christ, I terminate the spirit of alcohol addiction in the life of any member of my church now in Jesus' name.
10. Under the covering of the blood of Jesus, I subdue and destroy any drug addiction, nicotine addiction, weed smoking, and any induced form of drugs out of the members of my church in Jesus' name.

DAY 8

The Heavy Burdens

Is not this the fast that I have chosen? to loose the bands of wickedness, to undo the heavy burdens, and to let the oppressed go free, and that ye break every yoke?
– Isaiah 58:6

DAY 8 – The Heavy Burdens

When the heavy burdens are not lifted in our lives, the cares and burdens of the world choke out the Word. God's Word will no longer be operating in our lives. Jesus spoke that it was not only the cares of this world that choked out the Word of God, but also the deceitfulness of riches.

LOG-ON: DAY 8 – Morning Prayers

Stand on these prayer points for at least five minutes and pray:

1. Under the covering of the Superior Blood of Jesus Christ, I declare today that anyone in my life (insert name of person) with an addiction problem receive total emancipation through the Living Blood of Jesus Christ.
2. Under the covering of the Superior Blood of Jesus Christ, I declare that the walls of my church shall be a Haven for those who are cast out and downtrodden in their family and society because of any form of addiction.
3. Under the covering of the Superior Blood of Jesus Christ, I declare that no child in my house, and my church will suffer what their parents suffered through addiction in Jesus' name.
4. Under the covering of the Superior Blood of Jesus Christ, I declare that no child in my church, and my family will inherit any bad habit from their parents in the name of Jesus.
5. Under the covering of the Superior Blood of Jesus Christ, I announce and proclaim divine breakthrough, and liberty in any family (insert names) that is suffering from substance abuse in Jesus' name.
6. Under the covering of the Superior Blood of Jesus

Christ, I induce and inject restoration, peace, and unity into every broken home represented in my church, and in my family in Jesus' name.
7. Under the covering of the Superior Blood of Jesus Christ, You that heareth prayer, may you liberate with immediate effect by the dynamic power of the Blood of Jesus anyone in my church, and my family who is struggling to quit drugs and any form of immorality in Jesus' name.
8. Under the covering of the Superior Blood of Jesus Christ, I boldly confess that my great commission has come, my change has come, my transformation is here, my lifting has come, new things are happening in my life, this is my time and my season, I shall never remain the same again in Jesus' name.
9. Under the covering of the Blood of Jesus Christ, I command an immediate transfer of wealth and power from the treasures of darkness into the bank accounts and control of the true prophets and people of God, to advance the purposes of God; spread the Gospel; win souls for Jesus, and establish His Kingdom on Earth (Isaiah 45:3).
10. Under the covering of the Blood of Jesus Christ, I command that every false prophet and those who subvert the purposes of God for the church, be uncovered and thrown down. I invoke the written judgments of God against Jezebel and her accomplices (Isaiah 47).

DAY 8

The Heavy Burdens

Is not this the fast that I have chosen? to loose the bands of wickedness, to undo the heavy burdens, and to let the oppressed go free, and that ye break every yoke? – Isaiah 58:6

THERE IS NO PROBLEM so big that Yahweh cannot solve it. There is not a problem so complex or powerful that Yahweh cannot handle it. The scripture tells us that Yahweh is omniscient; He is all knowing, and omnipotent; all powerful.

All the wisdom of the world is His. Beyond that, the scripture tells us that Yahweh says the fast that I have chosen is: *"to undo the heavy burdens" (Isaiah 58:6).*

The word, "burdens" is the Hebrew word, "aguddah" which translates as, band, binding, cords, or bands. So, the wording here means "to unfasten the cords of the yoke," to set something free from a kind of slavery (bondage).

What is referred to here are things in the soul that influence the direction of our lives. The older animal dictates the direction for the younger animal. The younger ox is compelled to follow the pace of the older ox. In the same way, the heavy burdens in your soul inspire bad decisions that cause you to stagnate in certain areas of your life or go around in circles. They sabotage your best intentions for progress.

Beloved, your heavy burden could be memories of painful experiences, destructive habits, wrong priorities, negative thought patterns, and offense toward God for a loss or disappointment. These weights hinder the proper functioning of your soul and frustrate the pursuit of your dreams. Sometimes these heavy burdens are the lies you have believed about yourself. Bad decisions and choices can also become weights in your soul, particularly the ones you are ignorant of. These heavy burdens in your soul when allowed to thrive, will make you go through life feeling weighed down. They create a sense of powerlessness and hopelessness about the possibility of change in your soul. And make you feel indifferent toward the truth of God's Word in certain areas of your life.

There are some things that people carry, that can become a heavy burden. There are situations and problems at work, or in families that become a burden. You wake up in the morning and you feel it. You go to bed at night and you are thinking about it. It may be that your life is so tangled up that it is a hopeless case for men. It may feel like your finances are completely messed up. You may have legal problems. You may have problems that are heavy. It may seem like your marriage is in shambles. I challenge you with the Word today: the solution is to call out to God during times of prayer and fasting.

When it seems hopeless, when it seems as if there is no way out, He will be the Way-Maker! Yahweh can deal with things in an instant that you have stressed over for weeks and months! Expect divine revelation! Expect the power of Yahweh to be revealed.

I have discovered in my own personal fasting that it takes about three to five days after I begin to fast for my mind and spirit to clear up. Then I receive clarity before the Lord. It is as though I hear His voice stronger and clearer. This will happen for you as well.

Child of God, what is the heavy burden in your heart? Are you weighed down at the thought of it? I have good news for you. You can undo the heavy burden.

Yahweh has the solution for your heavy burden:

> *"Come unto me (an invitation) all ye that labour and are heavy laden and I will give you rest. Take my yoke upon you and learn of me for I am meek and lowly in heart and ye shall find rest unto your souls. For my yoke is easy and my burden is light."*
> *– Matthew 11:28-30*

Our LORD Jesus is the lifter and destroyer of heavy burdens. In this verse of scripture, He spoke about heavy burdens. Unbeknown to many people, they are carrying heavy loads on their heads. These are not physical loads, but spiritually, they have been given something to carry that is weighing them down in life. Many have yokes upon them but they do not know. There are people who are laboring under demonic bondages. There are those who are carrying heavy burdens. Do you feel overwhelmed in life? Do you feel like giving up? Are you tired of this life? These are all indications that there is a heavy burden sitting on your head. The enemy the devil has set a heavy load upon the neck of many individuals. The good news is that there is a yoke breaker; His name is Jesus Christ, the one who can break the yoke and remove the burden. When He has finished removing the burden and breaking the yoke, He will give you His own yoke and place His burden upon you. His own yoke is easy and His own burden is light.

We are to believe that in this stage of our fasting, there is power to break every yoke. The anointing of God is present to destroy the yoke:

> *And it shall come to pass in that day, that his burden shall be taken away from off thy shoulder, and his yoke from off thy neck, and the yoke shall be destroyed because of the anointing.*
>
> – Isaiah 10:27

⇒ TIPS FOR TODAY
1. Break every yoke of limitation and curses imputed over your bloodline.
- Pray for all your family members and friends that they'll find peace and liberty through the saving power of Jesus Christ.

2. Prayer that heavy burdens will be removed from your life.
- Let your star begin to shine after today.
- Pray and make prophetic declarations over your head.
- Christ is your head, therefore you shall not carry any heavy burdens.

PRAYER GUIDE 8:
- Pray for the anointing that destroys yokes and unloads all heavy burdens.
- Pray for the removal every burden in your bloodline: mention those burdens by name if you know them.
- Pray against family limitations such as genetic diseases in your family and age limitation in the bloodline.

LOG-OFF: DAY 8 – Evening Prayers

Stand on these prayer points for at least five minutes and pray:

1. Under the covering of the Superior Blood of Jesus Christ, I declare: no weapon that is formed against me shall prosper.

2. Under the covering of the Superior Blood of Jesus Christ, I confess: in righteousness I am established. I am far from oppression, for I shall not fear and from terror for it shall not come near me.

3. Under the covering of the Superior Blood of Jesus Christ, I believe and confess: the Lord shall cover me with His feathers, because I have made Him my dwelling place.

4. Under the covering of the Superior Blood of Jesus Christ, I boldly declare: evil shall not befall me. I shall tread upon the Lion and the Cobra and surely the Lord will always deliver me from the snare of the fowlers. God has made me a beneficiary of divine health through the stripes that were laid on Jesus Christ.

5. Under the covering of the Superior Blood of Jesus Christ, I believe and declare: through Jesus Christ I have access to the throne of grace of God, to find peace with God.

6. Under the covering of the Superior Blood of Jesus Christ, I believe and confess: I have prosperity, for God will no longer withhold any good thing from me.

7. Under the covering of the Superior Blood of Jesus Christ, I have spoken with the tongue of the learned

and as it is written, I shall be justified by the words of my mouth.

8. Under the covering of the Superior Blood of Jesus Christ, I ask that the Word of God I have confessed begin to transform me to the original image God designed me to be in His Book.

9. Under the covering of the Superior Blood of Jesus Christ, I ask that the blood of Jesus wipe away every mark of reproach, whether physical or spiritual.

10. Under the covering of the Blood of Jesus Christ, I ask for the blood of Jesus to erase every evil and negative name I was ever called.

DAY 9

Freedom from Oppression

Is not this the fast that I have chosen? to loose the bands of wickedness, to undo the heavy burdens, and to let the oppressed go free, and that ye break every yoke?
Isaiah 58:6

DAY 9: Freedom from Oppression

May you receive divine grace, empowerment and the tenacity of the Spirit of God to progress through this fasting. One of the most dangerous spirits that roams the earth today is the Spirit of the Oppressor. In this ninth day of our fast, we will channel the power of Yahweh to enforce angelic destruction against any spirit of the oppressor in our lives, and amongst our loved ones and family.

LOG-ON: DAY 9 – Morning Prayers

Enter these prayer points (Use each prayer point to pray for at least five minutes):

1. Under the covering of the Superior Blood of the Living Christ, every seed of oppression in my life be destroyed by Holy Spirit fire, in the name of Jesus.
2. Under the covering of the Superior Blood of the Living Christ, O God, arise and do something in my life today that will confound my adversaries, in the name of Jesus.
3. Under the covering of the Superior Blood of the Living Christ, every design of oppression, I terminate you now, in the name of Jesus.
4. Under the covering of the Superior Blood of the Living Christ, thou power of witchcraft oppression, be destroyed now, in the name of Jesus.
5. Under the covering of the Superior Blood of the Living Christ, Holy Ghost fire, sanitize my body, soul and spirit, against the spirit of oppression in the name of Jesus.
6. Under the covering of the Superior Blood of the Living Christ, I fire back every arrow of oppression back to the sender, in the name of Jesus.

7. Under the covering of the Superior Blood of the Living Christ, every yoke of oppression, break, in the name of Jesus.
8. Under the covering of the Superior Blood of the Living Christ, O God, arise and let every power of oppression scatter, in the name of Jesus.
9. Under the covering of the Superior Blood of the Living Christ, every weapon of oppression fashioned against me, be destroyed now, in the name of Jesus.
10. Under the covering of the Superior Blood of the Living Christ, any power that wants me to die in this condition, die, in the name of Jesus.

DAY 9
Freedom from Oppression

Is not this the fast that I have chosen? to loose the bands of wickedness, to undo the heavy burdens, and to let the oppressed go free, and that ye break every yoke?– Isaiah 58:6

YAHWEH IS TELLING US, the fast He has chosen is *"to let the oppressed go free"* (Isaiah 58:6c).

I know one thing is that if you are a true believer you cannot be possessed by the devil. However, you can be oppressed. Have you ever just felt a heaviness upon you? Have you ever felt like you couldn't get a breakthrough? Do you ever feel like you don't have the authority to fight your way out of a wet paper bag?

It is the oppression of the enemy. Yahweh says that He wants you to be free from oppression. Yahweh wants you to have victory. God wants your family, your friends, and your neighbors to be free.

Fasting increases your capacity to praise God and praising Him will cause all heaviness to leave. Fasting increases your faith level. Fasting brings victory over the spirit of heaviness and oppression. Fasting opens your eyes to the needs of a lost and dying world around you.

It is necessary to pause here for a moment, and speak on this subject of oppression. Oppression affects so many in the Church, as well as so many in the secular world. The Spirit of Oppression is grossly underestimated by the Church of the Lord Jesus Christ in this hour. Its effects are far reaching, and varied.

So, what is oppression?

The Hebrew word for "oppression" is "osheq" (pronounced o-shek), meaning oppression, extortion (to obtain from a person by force, intimidation, or undue illegal power, cruelly). The Merriam-Webster's Collegiate Dictionary defines "oppression" as unjust or cruel exercise of authority or power; it is a sense of being weighed down in body or mind; depression.

When a person is oppressed, they just cannot seem to get up or get ahead, no matter what they do. Oppression can affect certain areas in a person's life, or their lives as a whole. There are multitudes of Christians, as well as people in the world who are being oppressed in some way or another. For example, the lack of results in ministry, unfruitful prayers, constant lack, or cycles of job failures, are often due to a spirit of oppression. Just when it seems like you are coming out of debt, then you lose your job, or an unexpected bill pops up. This is the spirit of oppression at work. Just when you are preparing to do ministry, then those who you were going to minister to, cannot come. We must not ignore this spirit, for it has long held down the people of God. If you get this truth in your spirit today, it will change your life.

There are many times in the life of a Christian when they are oppressed. Yes, the child of God can be oppressed. Not only can an individual be oppressed, but ministries, churches, families, cities, nations and an entire race of people can be oppressed as well. The enemy tries to overwhelm Christians with things, issues, troubles, burdens, lack, and so forth, causing oppression. After long terms or extended times of oppression, the Christian can then become depressed. Oppression is caused by external circumstances, while depression is rooted in the thoughts of the individual, who constantly considers the external things, thus causing them to be internalized.

You Have Been Given Power Over The Spirit of Oppression.

It is our responsibility to come against this spirit: *Is not this the fast that I have chosen...to let the oppressed go free. (Isaiah 58:6).*

I often hear Christians petitioning Yahweh for His power, but with Yahweh's power comes responsibility. Yahweh extends to us His power for His purposes. When we look at the life of Jesus, we must seek to do those things that He did, as He said we would in John 14:12-14. In Acts 10:38 we see some of the things that Jesus did. It reads:

> *How God anointed Jesus of Nazareth with the Holy Ghost and with power: who went about doing good, and healing all that were oppressed of the devil; for God was with him.*

It is our responsibility to deliver those oppressed of the devil. Yet, because we are oppressed, we cannot focus on the work that we, the Church, are called to do. Those who are oppressed are captives in some capacity, who must be set free. We must throw this spirit off of ourselves, and then we will be free to go and deliver many in Jesus' name who are also being held captive by this spirit.

The Purpose and Designs of the Spirit of Oppression.

The purpose of oppression is to hold down. As I have stated earlier, long term oppression causes depression (within a person), with the intent to cause regression (people to go backward). Whenever you try to move forward in God and receive His promises, then the enemy uses oppression as a weapon against you, to try and get you to go back or regress (return to an earlier or worse condition).

It is the purpose of the spirit of oppression to not only overburden someone with issues, but also to cause them to be too stuffed, busy or depressed to employ the God ordained strategies necessary to bring them out. Oppression discourages. Oppression is like a cloak that is put upon a person. Yet, unless that person does a wardrobe change, that person will not come out.

Isaiah 61:3 speaks of this wardrobe change, it says:

> *To appoint unto them that mourn in Zion, to give unto them beauty for ashes, the oil of joy for mourning, the garment of praise for the spirit of heaviness; that they might be called trees of righteousness, the planting of the LORD, that he might be glorified.*

Recently I have been crying out to the Lord, because I have felt oppressed. So much it seems was on me. Yet the provisions to accomplish the vision that I was sure the LORD had given me was not there. It was at this point that I would either have to downsize the vision that God gave me, or throw off the cloak of oppression and praise and glorify

God. So often in the past I had battled aggressively with this spirit in its various forms and shapes. I have found that at these times when I cry out to Yahweh for deliverance, He does not move on my behalf to deliver me. Rather there seems to be silence from Heaven. Sometimes, I am so overwhelmed by responsibilities, lack of provisions, and so forth, that I raise my level of weeping and crying out to Yahweh, yet the force of the oppressor intensifies with equal resistance to my prayers. At times, I will express my prayers in protruded lamentations to Yahweh, in great distress. Still there is silence from Heaven. It is at this point that many lose their faith. It is only when I stop weeping unnecessarily, when I stop complaining in prayers and pick up, and employ Yahweh's Biblical strategies which I had all along, that I begin to see some breakthrough.

When trying to get an understanding of oppression, you must know that it is both a spirit and a weapon. Yes, oppression is a spirit that is used as a weapon against you. It is formed against you (designed specifically to be advantageous against you) based on your particular weaknesses or bents. Demonic entities observe you to see how they can find a doorway to oppress you. When they find the right doorway of sin, or disobedience, then they form an oppressive weapon to use in that area against you.

Yet, we must always remember Isaiah 54:17, which says;

> *No weapon that is formed against thee shall prosper; and every tongue that shall rise against thee in judgment thou shalt condemn. This is the heritage of the servants of the LORD, and their righteousness is of me, saith the LORD.*

Oppression should not be able to prosper against you. But to stop it, you must shut the doors that it would operate through. I want you to understand something. The greater the call, the greater the work, the greater Yahweh's purposed breakthrough for you, then the greater the oppression and resistance from the enemy.

The Symptoms That The Spirit of Oppression Is Operational In Your Life.

Many Christians don't think that they are important enough for the enemy to take the time to design weaponry to specifically stop them. Stop looking at what you are presently doing, and begin to see Yahweh's desired purpose in your life. The enemy has designed weapons against you, not because of what you are doing now, but rather for the potential you have when you fully embrace Yahweh's purpose for your life. Many confuse the operations of the spirit of oppression with being cursed. Although curses can use oppression to enforce its objective, oppression can also work outside of a curse as a weapon against people. One way to identify the operation of a spirit of oppression, is when you first start out doing something you find success, then all of a sudden, things dry up. This can often signify that a spirit of oppression has stepped in to be a weapon to resist you and what you have been given or called to do. The enemy uses the spirit of oppression as a weapon against you to do many things, some of which are:

- *Hinder your finances and provisions* - Living from hand to mouth, pay check to pay check, barely getting by. Each time that it seems you are getting ahead, then something else comes up to hinder you from having enough. Over and over again this may happen.
- *Stop people from getting saved or coming to the Lord* - They can oppress individuals, families, communities, cities, nations, ethnic groups causing people not to get saved or to come to Christ for salvation. They will oppress people from getting saved to cause you to be discouraged and stop trying

to evangelize. One day you may talk to a person and they seem interested in Jesus Christ, yet the next day they don't want to hear anything about Him. It is a good possibility that the spirit of oppression used someone to discourage them from coming to Christ, thus oppressing their salvation.

- *Frustrate the growth of a church or ministry* - When you know that Yahweh has called you to do a certain ministry service for Him, and you don't see breakthrough or your ministry may be shut down or have limited results, it might be the enemy oppressing people from responding.
- *Stop opportunity for advancement and promotion* - You may have favor with a job when you first start, then things go downhill from there. You see those who are not as skilled as you being promoted above and before you. They are holding or pressing down your opportunities.
- *Oppress healing and deliverance* - You quote the Word, and believe in healing, yet the manifestation does not come. These oppressive spirits are trying to hold down and oppress the manifestation of God's healing and deliverance power in your life.
- *Oppress the Anointing from flowing when a person is ministering* - They can oppress the speaker, singer, or the people who you are ministering to. They may use fear, doubt, sleepiness, etcetera to cause the Anointing to cease from flowing.
- *Oppress families, causing issues* - Your family may always be broken, never having peace. Perhaps one issue after another rises up in your family. This may be a way the enemy uses to oppress you, through family issues and troubles.
- *Oppress breakthrough in a community, people groups (including youth, women, men, etc)* - The spirit of oppression can target individual groups and categories of people to oppress them. He can lead them to sin, and then oppress them. Such is the case

with many communities that have a lack of men (due to imprisonment, etc.), or with the youth, trying to get them to pursue some fantasy of becoming famous so that they can be worshipped.

- *Oppress your health and strength* - Sometimes you can feel exhausted or weak, yet you know that you have rested. Many people wake up tired. This should not be. There is a possibility that oppression is at work to stop you from having the strength to be a testimony for the Living God.
- *Oppress your name by slander* - The enemy can oppress you by discrediting or slandering your name and your character falsely.
- *Oppress your time with issues and problems (especially other people's issues)* - You could have planned to spend time in prayer, when the enemy has someone call you with a supposed emergency, all with the purpose of oppressing your time.
- *Oppress your faith to believe Yahweh* - These spirits try to hold down and stop your faith to believe Yahweh. They want you to doubt that Yahweh is doing what you have asked Him to do.
- *Oppress breakthrough in your life* - Wherever you have been striving to get a breakthrough the enemy pushes down, with hopes that you accept where you are and what you have, yet with the intentions to take even that from you.
- *Oppress people from being baptized in the Holy Spirit* - So many Christians are seeking the Baptism of the Holy Spirit, yet many never receive it. Why? The enemy tries in many ways to oppress them. It could be through doubt, fear, anxiety, etcetera.
- *Oppress dreams and revelation from the Lord* - Just as with the Prophet Daniel, whose answer from Yahweh through an Angel was delayed (oppressed) because of demonic activity, so can your dreams,

and revelations from Yahweh be delayed and
hindered as well.
- *Oppress understanding of the Word of
  Yahweh* - Some find it difficult to memorize or study
  the Word of Yahweh. Sleep seems to come upon
  some as soon as they open up the Word. I have
  heard some Christians say, "whenever I can't get to
  sleep, I just open up my Bible and soon I fall right to
  sleep." This is because a demonic spirit wants to
  oppress them from reading the life-giving Word of
  Yahweh.
- *Oppress the Gifts of the Holy Spirit from operating
  in people's lives* - They oppress the Gifts from
  operating in the lives of the Christian. This can be a
  confidence or faith issue, it can be a fear issue, yet in
  any case it is oppression holding them down.
- *Oppress you from getting into prayer* - These spirits
  try to oppress the Christian from getting into the
  presence of Yahweh. They cause all kinds of issues
  and distractions to push down a person's time and
  ability to seek God's face.

The enemy uses a variety of tools to oppress the people of Yahweh, and others. They can use fear to oppress, lack to oppress, sickness to oppress, other people to oppress you with their words or opinions (this can happen through people picking on you, discouraging you, or making everything that you do or are called to do seem like nothing), peer pressure to oppress, low self-esteem to oppress, prejudice or racism to oppress you, doubt and unbelief to oppress you, pride to oppress you, and more.

So many people are praising Yahweh and praising Yahweh for a breakthrough, over, and over again, yet that breakthrough does not happen. Why? Often it is oppression that is holding it up or pressing it down. The garment of praise increases our faith, for in praising Yahweh we put in view His divine attributes, thus giving us greater faith and confidence in Him. Yet, that should not be the only weapon or tool that we use here. Praise can bring in Yahweh's presence and send the enemy fleeing, but when we stop praising, they come back. The proper tool to use here is binding and casting out the Spirit of Oppression. This is how we resist them, causing them to flee from us. James 4:7 says:

> *Submit yourselves therefore to God. Resist the devil, and he will flee from you.*

Whether you have asked for something in faith, or praised Yahweh for the manifestation, sometimes it might yet require that you bind the Spirit of Oppression off of those things that you have asked and praised Yahweh for. Yahweh can give you a ministry and a specific vision on how to fulfill it, and it still does not manifest, because the Spirit of Oppression has come against you. Cast this spirit out, and then keep it out and watch the manifestation of Yahweh's promises break forth in your life.

The Mission Of The Spirit Of Oppression Is To Kill Your Faith In Yahweh.

The enemy wants to oppress you until you begin to doubt and thus not believe Yahweh regarding who you are in Him, or what He has called you to do.

It is imperative that when you are warring against the spirit of oppression that you balance the warfare with fasting. Often while you are warring against this spirit it sneaks up behind you to attack your faith, and unless you enter into a state of fasting, you might lose focus. It is the spirit of oppression's goal to have you lose your faith, first in the fact that Yahweh does answer you, second, in the fact that Yahweh does care, and thirdly, it wants you to ultimately lose your faith in the fact that there is a God. You must keep and strengthen your faith in these times by intense fasting.

After this you must praise God for who He is (His faithfulness, love, mercy, etcetera). Often, we get so busy with the warfare (especially when we begin to see success in it), that we forget the area of faith, in which the enemy then attacks.

The Spirit of Oppression will always try to get you to look at its effects against you. You must not look at what this demonic spirit is attempting to do against you. This will cause your faith to decay. You can never try to believe Yahweh based on what you are seeing; rather you must believe Him based on the truth of who He is. Your ministry will never rise above where and what you can believe Yahweh for, before you see it. This applies to dealing with oppression as well. You will never remove this spirit, if you will not believe that you are battling it. Demonic spirits want to make you think that you are not doing anything to stop them in your spiritual warfare. Do not stop warring, for you are making progress.

You must engage this spirit, or else you will stay oppressed. Doing nothing is not an option. For in your inactivity against it, it will actively come against you to continue to press you down, until you are crushed. Many Christians, instead of consistently fighting this spirit, they rather fall into its trap of looking at the results of what it is doing against them, and then begin to complain and murmur about their plight. Fight the good fight of faith and do not fall into the sin of complaining, for it will give this spirit further access to oppress you.

You Cannot Fight The Spirit Of Oppression In Unrighteousness!

Do not take this particular point lightly, for if you do, you will become an unnecessary spiritual warfare casualty, "you cannot war in unrighteousness!" Isaiah 54:14 says:

> *In righteousness shalt thou be established: thou shalt be far from oppression; for thou shalt not fear: and from terror; for it shall not come near thee.*

It is in righteousness that you are established, causing oppression to not be able to overcome you, for in righteousness it has no legal place to press you down. You see, to retaliate against you, this spirit will need a place of sin (whether little or great), and if there is none in you, it will try and cause you to sin to create a legal way for it to oppress you. To defeat this spirit, you must stay in right standing. You will not defeat this spirit by falling into old habits of sin, including little sins like complaining, gossiping, lusting, lying, fantasizing about ungodly things, etcetera. You must stay holy both in your mind and in your actions.

It Is Only In Consistency and Persistence Can You Win.

To defeat this enemy, you are required to be constant and persistent in your battle against it. Daily, you must repent of your sins and bind the Spirit of Oppression off of yourself and everything under your authority. Bind it off of each individual thing that the Lord leads you to. Not just once in a while; rather daily, as well as throughout each day.

As I have stated earlier, when battling this spirit, please be aware that it will respond by sending things and people at you to oppress you from warring against it. For example, if you are binding a Spirit of Oppression off of your finances, then it may respond by sending more bills at you, or unexpected things that will require you to spend more money. Its purpose in doing this is to get you to complain, doubt, fear, etcetera; which will give it a place to legally come at you and re-oppress you as you are climbing out.

Spirits of Oppression constantly try to get you to look at the results of what they have done or are doing against you presently. Do not dare think that they are greater than Yahweh. Bind them and begin to thank Yahweh for what He has done (especially what you have asked Yahweh for concerning the areas the enemy has oppressed). Beloved you must constantly war against these spirits to gain ground, for they are always contesting you. Little by little you will see their effects dwindle, and the manifestation of Yahweh's provisions and promises break forth.

Again, as you begin to war against these spirits, they will fight tooth and nail to stop you from getting results. Yet you must press forward past its wall of resistance, moving one brick of oppression at a time, until full breakthrough is manifested. You must not be moved by this spirit; rather you must be persistent and constant in your warfare against it to move it. I regularly bind and war against the Spirit of oppression. Daily I do this for the breakthroughs I know I need.

These spirits do all they can to stop you. A few days before I started work on this book, I started experiencing some bizarre discomfort in my body, and spirit. I was not in the mood to write, read, or think. In fact, my mind was completely deprived of even the ability to recall a single verse of scripture. Indeed, it was depressing, one of the worst states I ever found myself in. Then as though that wasn't enough, about three days later, the flu began to work its way in me. It was at this point, I discerned the enemy, this spirit called oppression, was on a mission to crush my ability to make any meaningful progress in my life. I was standing before the bathroom sink when this revelation suddenly entered my spirit, and without hesitation, I prayed, "O LORD, I bind this spirit, I curse this sickness, I receive my deliverance with immediate effect. I shall write and complete this book this week." Dear friend, at that very instance, without exaggerating this story, there was an immediate release in my spirit. I felt a presence lifted off me. I was immediately sound in my mind and I knew of a certainty that I had been delivered of something. The next day, I sat down to write, and I did so for hours without struggle. This is why I am taking the liberty to spend time in this book to help you deal with this stubborn spirit.

Child of God, you must prepare for war against this spirit, as well as others. You must be constant in fighting this enemy that seeks to keep you and all your loved ones pressed down.

The Challenge.

I challenge you to combat the Spirit of Oppression for the rest of this year. If you commit to this and succeed you will see great breakthroughs in your life and calling. Start by doing this during this fasting phase:

- Repent of all of your sins. Never go into battle with the enemy with doors open, for they will use them to afflict you.
- Stay out of sin, and when you sin repent quickly.
- Each day go to war against the Spirit of Oppression. You may be required to do it several times a day.
- Quote scripture when binding and casting out this spirit; such as Mark 16:17-18, which says: *"And these signs shall follow them that believe; In my name shall they cast out devils; they shall speak with new tongues; They shall take up serpents; and if they drink any deadly thing, it shall not hurt them; they shall lay hands on the sick, and they shall recover."*
- List the things that you are binding this spirit off of (your finances, home, marriage, children, job, opportunities, ministry, church, extended family, souls being saved, the Baptism of the Holy Spirit manifesting in your life, etcetera). Daily take at least

fifteen minutes or more warring against this spirit. Do not forget to bind the spirits that oppression tries to use against you as you war against it, such as; spirits of doubt, fear, unbelief, complaining, retaliation, etcetera.

You must be persistent until you see the breakthrough. Even after you see it, continue to bind this spirit in order to keep the breakthrough.

LOG-OFF: DAY 9 – Evening Prayers

Enter these prayer points before you go to bed (Use each prayer point to pray for at least five minutes):

1. Under the covering of the Superior Blood of Jesus, every inherited oppression, be terminated now, in the name of Jesus.
2. Under the covering of the Superior Blood of Jesus, every evil power that pursued my parents and is now pursing me, expire now, in the name of Jesus.
3. Under the covering of the Superior Blood of Jesus, every power that has vowed to destroy me, be terminated by the Holy Ghost fire now, in the name of Jesus.
4. Under the covering of the Superior Blood of Jesus, within seven days, let any stubborn spirit of oppression in my life be consumed by the Holy Ghost fire, in the name of Jesus.
5. Under the covering of the Superior Blood of Jesus, arrows of affliction, backfire by fire, in Jesus' name.
6. Under the covering of the Superior Blood of Jesus, every yoke of the oppressor, break, in the Jesus' name.
7. Under the covering of the Superior Blood of Jesus, every yoke of foundational curse, break, in Jesus' name.
8. Under the covering of the Superior Blood of Jesus, I claim every good thing my dreams reveal.
9. Under the covering of the Superior Blood of Jesus, I expel every evil power attached to my name, in the name of Jesus.
10. Under the covering of the Superior Blood of Jesus, thou power of darkness representing, impersonating or bearing my name in the spirit realm receive divine judgment now, in the name of Jesus.

DAY 10
The Yoke Breaker

Is not this the fast that I have chosen? to loose the bands of wickedness, to undo the heavy burdens, and to let the oppressed go free, and that ye break every yoke? – Isaiah 58:6

DAY 10: The Yoke Breaker

LOG-ON: DAY 10 – Morning Prayers

Enter these prayer points (Use each prayer point to pray for at least five minutes):

1. Under the covering of the Superior Blood of Jesus Christ, Yoke Breaker, break every evil chain binding me to problems.
2. Under the covering of the Superior Blood of Jesus Christ, every satanic agenda assigned against my progress, scatter by fire, in the name of Jesus.
3. Under the covering of the Superior Blood of Jesus Christ, every weapon of affliction assigned against my life, backfire in the name of Jesus.
4. Under the covering of the Superior Blood of Jesus Christ, every yoke of stagnancy in my life break now.
5. Under the covering of the Superior Blood of Jesus Christ, any spirit of oppression frustrating my vision, I rebuke you, in the name of Jesus.
6. Under the covering of the Superior Blood of Jesus Christ, every power harboring enchantment against me, fall down and perish in Jesus' name.
7. Under the covering of the Superior Blood of Jesus Christ, every satanic prayer uttered against me, I declare it shall not stand in Jesus' name.
8. Under the covering of the Superior Blood of Jesus Christ, any spirit of oppression working to frustrate my focus, I rebuke you by the blood of Jesus.
9. Under the covering of the Superior Blood of Jesus Christ, every evil altar and demonic provocateurs using evil chains to manipulate my life, I rebuke you.
10. Under the covering of the Superior Blood of Jesus Christ, every evil chain tying me down, break and burn to ashes in the name of Jesus.

DAY 10

The Yoke Breaker

Is not this the fast that I have chosen? to loose the bands of wickedness, to undo the heavy burdens, and to let the oppressed go free, and that ye break every yoke? – Isaiah 58:6

Do you reign over your emotions, or do your emotions reign over you?

Consider Isaiah 58:6: *"And that you break every yoke?"* A yoke is put on oxen to control them. A yoke is put on oxen so that the one who is driving the oxen can steer them in the direction the driver wants them to go. Yahweh wants us to be free from every yoke but His. What is driving you?

- Some people allow their emotions to drive them.
- Some people are driven by stress.
- Some people allow anger to drive them.

- Some people are driven to depression and despair by negative thoughts.

Yahweh wants us to have joy, peace, hope, and courage as we face life's obstacles. Some have found themselves in situations where it seems like the enemy says, "to the right" and they go right. The enemy says, "go left" and they go left. They are under his yoke. It affects their emotions and mental state. Yahweh does not want you to live under that emotional strain. If you wake up in the morning and you are in tears, if you go to bed at night and you just aren't happy, it is time for every yoke to go. It is time that the only one who controls you is the Spirit of the Living God! The kingdom of heaven is not eat and drink but righteousness, peace and joy in the Holy Ghost.

God wants us free. And the key is fasting and prayer.

> *And it shall come to pass in that day, that his burden shall be taken away from off thy shoulder, and his yoke from off thy neck, and the yoke shall be destroyed because of the anointing.– Isaiah 10:27*

There is a yoke-breaking anointing. Yahweh tells us in the Bible that "I will make a way where there is no way" (Isaiah 43:16-19). There is a facility of escape. Man's word is not final because man is never bigger than Yahweh.

What Is A Yoke?

- A satanic instrument of oppression used to limit a person's growth, fulfillment, destiny, breakthrough, etcetera. It is a hindering barrier, from the Hebrew word, *"mowtah."*

- A satanic device that sponsors affliction in the lives of people. The scribe in 1 Kings 12:11 explains it powerfully in this illustration:

    > *And now whereas my father did lade you with a heavy yoke, I will add to your yoke: my father hath chastised you with whips, but I will chastise you with scorpions.*

    Dear friend, you cannot negotiate with Satan. The dark places of this earth are full of the habitation of cruelty. You must pray with above average intensity.

- A yoke is something that places the destiny of a person in the hands of the enemy. A prisoner cannot eat what he pleases or go anywhere he wants to. In Acts 12:6, we are told that Peter was in prison between two soldiers bound with two chains and there were keepers who kept the prison door. The only thing that could free the destiny of Peter was a divine intervention. I declare emphatically and prophetically that, you will be released today, in Jesus' name.

The Bible tells us in Deuteronomy 15:1 that *"at the end of every seven years thou shall make a release."* As you go through this fasting phase, I speak prophetically in the pages of this book without any fear of demonic contradictions that, this is your season of release in Jesus' name.

That yoke placed upon your life from childhood is broken this very moment:

> *For thou hast broken the yoke of his burden, and the staff of his shoulder, the rod of his oppressor, as in the day of Midian. For every battle of the warrior is with confused noise, and garments rolled in blood; but this shall be with burning and fuel of fire.*
> *– Isaiah 9:4-5*

In Isaiah 9:4-5 above, God said this battle shall be with burning and fuel of fire. By the tokens of the spoken Word, may the zeal of the LORD of Host perform this for you in Jesus' name.

What Are The Symptoms Of Destiny Yokes?

- When you are enduring life instead of enjoying it. This is a gradual resignation to fate. You wish life could end sooner for you. This is not the will of God.
- When you are marking time instead of making time fruitful.
- When you don't feel like yourself. You feel you're under the control of someone or something.
- When you are carrying a load. Joseph's brothers carried a load on their heads plus an extra load they knew nothing about. They walked a great distance only to be told to turn back because of the extra load that was put in their luggage, which they knew nothing about! You're always carrying people's problems. You are always getting hurt and in pain when it's no fault of your own.
- You have no direction in life. Life is stagnant for you. Everyone is racing past you.
- When you can't see the next 10 – 20 years (visions, dreams) and have confidence that it will be well.
- When the journey of 40 days is taking 40 years.
- When your wellbeing is under ceaseless attack. You feel restless, often in poor health and fall quickly into mood swings.

Why Is Jesus A Yoke Breaker?

1. He broke the yoke of profitless hard labor and near-success syndrome in the life of the man at the pool called Bethesda (John 5:8). This man had diverse, multi-dimensional yokes but one glorious day Jesus said to him *"rise, take up thy bed, and walk!"* The problem of 38 years got solved in 38 seconds! Jesus, the yoke breaker will visit you today!

2. He broke the yoke of premature death in the life of Lazarus (John 11:34). He broke the yoke of death, even His own death.

3. He is the carrier of the Breaker Anointing. In Malachi 2:13, the prophet declares: "The breaker is come up before them: they have broken up, and have passed through the gate, and are gone out by it: and their king shall pass before them, and the Lord on the head of them."

The Breaker Anointing is the catalytic deposit of the Holy Spirit, endued and consigned to all believers to destroy the yoke of the enemy, and fulfill God's mandate on the earth.

This type of anointing will break through every yoke and offload all burdens to the furtherance of the Gospel. It shakes every shackle loose, that holds individuals and the Church back from coming into their destiny and inheritance. Jesus promises that "the Kingdom suffers violence and the violent take it by force."

I announce to you prophetically that the Breaker's Anointing is activated in your life. May Yahweh have respect unto your words, honor your prayers, and may angels enforce your decrees without deliberations in Jesus' name.

LOG-OFF: DAY 10 – Evening Prayers

Enter these prayer points before you go to bed (Use each prayer point to pray for at least five minutes):

1. Under the covering of the Superior of Blood of Jesus Christ, Yoke Breaker, break every evil chain binding me to problems.
2. Under the covering of the Superior of Blood of Jesus Christ, every satanic agenda assigned against my progress, I rebuke it, in the name of Jesus.
3. Under the covering of the Superior of Blood of Jesus Christ, every weapon of affliction assigned against my life, be destroyed in the name of Jesus.
4. Under the covering of the Superior of Blood of Jesus Christ, every yoke of stagnancy in my life break now.
5. Under the covering of the Superior of Blood of Jesus Christ, every yoke of darkness designed to restrict and hinder my destiny path, I destroy in the name of Jesus.
6. Under the covering of the Superior of Blood of Jesus Christ, I remove any yoke bound to my neck.
7. Under the covering of the Superior of Blood of Jesus Christ, I loose anyone in my family (mention names) bound to the yoke of stagnancy and unprofitable hands in Jesus' name.
8. Under the covering of the Superior of Blood of Jesus Christ, I declare my church is loosed from any yoke of stagnation in Jesus' name.
9. Under the covering of the Superior of Blood of Jesus Christ, I confess and declare I am anointed to break the yoke of bondage in my family in Jesus' name.
10. Under the covering of the Superior of Blood of Jesus Christ, I boldly confess and declare, this year I will see success, I will fulfill God's assignment in my life, and I will prosper in good health and in my finances in Jesus' name.

DAY 11
Inconvenient Giving

Is it not to deal thy bread to the hungry, and that thou bring the poor that are cast out to thy house? when thou seest the naked, that thou cover him; and that thou hide not thyself from thine own flesh?
Isaiah 58:7

DAY 11 – Inconvenient Giving

We have now reached the eleventh day of our fasting. Here we must capture God's principle of self-denial in order to be a blessing to others. A generous fast offering blesses others. When we bless others, God blesses us. Isaiah teaches the principle of fast offerings.

LOG-ON: DAY 11 – Morning Prayers

Enter these prayer points (Use each prayer point to pray for at least five minutes):

1. Under the covering of the Superior Blood of Jesus Christ, Father, come as light and illuminate the scriptures to me, in the name of Jesus.
2. Under the covering of the Superior Blood of Jesus Christ, Father, come as wind and blow away my sorrow, in the name of Jesus.
3. Under the covering of the Superior Blood of Jesus Christ, Father, come as fire, purify my heart, and consume any demonic plantations in my life, in the name of Jesus.
4. Under the covering of the Superior Blood of Jesus Christ, Father, come as water, wash me clean, and restore my life in the name of Jesus.
5. Under the covering of the Superior Blood of Jesus Christ, Father, come as a Leader, direct my every step, guide me to make the right decisions this year in the name of Jesus.
6. Under the covering of the Superior Blood of Jesus Christ, move by Your fire, O Lord, upon my disordered heart, in the name of Jesus.
7. Under the covering of the Superior Blood of Jesus Christ, O Lord, take away from my life all the

infirmities, and diabolical designs in the name of Jesus.
8. Under the covering of the Superior Blood of Jesus Christ, O Lord, take away from my life any spirit of hate and unholy jealousy, in the name of Jesus.
9. Under the covering of the Superior Blood of Jesus Christ, let the mists and darkness of unbelief be lifted away from me, in the name of Jesus.
10. Under the covering of the Superior Blood of Jesus Christ, O Lord, brighten my soul with the pure light of heaven so that I occupy my place in life, in the name of Jesus.

DAY 11

Inconvenient Giving

Is it not to deal thy bread to the hungry, and that thou bring the poor that are cast out to thy house? when thou seest the naked, that thou cover him; and that thou hide not thyself from thine own flesh?
Isaiah 58:7

WHEN YOU FAST, it makes you more compassionate for others who are hungry. Yahweh says the fast that I have chosen will concern those who are physically hungry.

Fasting involves denying yourself a meal or two. But God's fast is not just about denying *yourself* a meal, but taking what you deny yourself and giving it to *someone else* who needs it more than you.

It is one thing to deny yourself that last piece of chicken today and then turn around and have it tomorrow. It is another thing to give that piece of chicken to someone else. Do you deny yourself just for the sake of denying yourself? Or do you turn it into an opportunity to serve others?

The fast that pleases Yahweh is when we deny ourselves that food, but instead of storing it for another day, we give it to someone who needs it today. The fast from food is to empty our fridge of all food and give that food, along with the money we will have spent on groceries that week to the poor. This is the true fast; the fast that pleases Yahweh. It is the fast that Yahweh has chosen. Yahweh's fast is to give to the poor and needy what we cannot have.

We qualify for God's promised blessings and power as we care for all of His children in accordance with the fast He has chosen.

Moreover, let's look beyond the physical to discover what Yahweh wants us to see in the Spiritual. The use of the word bread in the Bible means "*food*". Another word used to describe food is meat. When Yahweh speaks of food He speaks of physical and Spiritual food.

When we fast we are directed to deal our bread to the hungry. The word deal (Hebrew: *"parac"*) means *"to break in pieces, to distribute"*. The hungry are those who are starving for the Word of God. The prophet Amos spoke of the day in which we live:

> *Behold, the days come, saith the Lord God, that I will send a famine in the land, not a famine of bread, nor a thirst for water, but of hearing the words of the Lord: And they shall wander from sea to sea, and from the north even to the east, they shall run to and fro to seek the word of the Lord, and shall not find it.– Amos 8:11-12*

There is a famine of hearing the Spiritual Word of Yahweh in the earth today. Man is running from coast to coast and from border to border looking for the true Word of God. Yahweh has given us the fast that we may hear His voice and receive direction, wisdom, and revelation. When we fast to hear the voice of Yahweh, He will speak His mysteries to us which have been hidden from the foundation of the earth (Romans 16:25).

When God reveals the mysteries to us in the fast, we are to distribute the Spiritual meat He has given us to those who are hungry for the deeper things of God. When Jesus expounded what is commonly referred to as the Lord's Prayer, He prayed:

> *"Give us this day our daily bread." – Matthew 6:11*

Our daily bread is the knowledge we accumulate from the Father on a daily basis. Jesus stated:

> *"I am that bread of life." – John 6:48*

Jesus is the bread and He came to reveal the Father to those who would receive Him. When we seek our daily bread, we are seeking to know Yahweh in a personal way. When we become partakers of the bread of life, then we become part of that one bread that Yahweh has in the earth. Paul wrote to the church at Corinth:

> *"For we being many are one bread, and one body: for we are all partakers of that one bread."*
> *– I Corinthians 10:17*

Those who are part of the one bread have become part of His one body who will partake of Christ Jesus in all His glory. Yahweh has given us the fast that we may hear from Him and break the bread of life from house to house as the early church did in the book of Acts. Yahweh is making those who will seek Him in fasting His ministers to distribute His Words of life, His revelations and His mysteries which He has hidden from the beginning of time. Yahweh has given the fast that we may receive from Him and break the bread of life with those who are in need.

What will God have you do during this fasting period? What will be the delight of God for you as you fast? What will cause God to favor you during this season of fasting and prayer?

⇒ **TIPS FOR TODAY**
God's delight is for us to Help the needy during this fast (vv. 7)

- Be generous during this fasting season.
- Give to the needy. Feed the hungry by the way side with discretion.
- Reconcile with any relatives who are in strife against you and help them if any have extended a hand for help.
- Be a peacekeeper and avoid inciting bitterness where you're called upon to help.

PRAYER GUIDE 11:
- Pray for people you know or meet who are in need of help in any form.
- Pray that God will make you a generous giver to the needy.
- Pray that God will strengthen your ability to tithe to Him and to give generously and cheerfully toward His work.
- Pray that you shall be a giver to the kingdom of Christ and never a borrower.
- Pray against the spirit of poverty and lack in your bloodline.

LOG-OFF: DAY 11 – Evening Prayers

Enter these prayer points before you go to bed (Use each prayer point in prayer for at least five minutes):

1. Under the covering of the Superior Blood of Jesus Christ, O Lord, uphold me, and I cannot fall, in the name of Jesus.
2. Under the covering of the Superior Blood of Jesus Christ, O Lord, strengthen me, and I cannot be moved, in the name of Jesus.
3. Under the covering of the Superior Blood of Jesus Christ, equip me, Lord, and I shall receive no destruction, in the name of Jesus.
4. Under the covering of the Superior Blood of Jesus Christ, stand by me, Lord, and Satan will depart, in the name of Jesus.
5. Under the covering of the Superior Blood of Jesus Christ, anoint my lips, O Lord, with a song of salvation, in the name of Jesus.
6. Under the covering of the Superior Blood of Jesus Christ, teach me, O Lord, to walk in your path, and be faithful to you, in the name of Jesus.
7. Under the covering of the Superior Blood of Jesus Christ, O Lord, water my soul richly with divine blessings, in the name of Jesus.
8. Under the covering of the Superior Blood of Jesus Christ, O Lord, give me a mountain-top-life, in the name of Jesus.
9. Under the covering of the Superior Blood of Jesus Christ, O Lord, make me a perfume of praiseful gratitude, in the name of Jesus.
10. Under the covering of the Superior Blood of Jesus Christ, O Lord, make me a happy holy person, in the name of Jesus.

DAY 12
Sacrificial Giving

Is it not to deal thy bread to the hungry, and that thou bring the poor that are cast out to thy house? when thou seest the naked, that thou cover him; and that thou hide not thyself from thine own flesh?
Isaiah 58:7

DAY 12 – Sacrificial Giving

This is day twelve of our fasting. We continue to manifest the power of self-denial during the fast. What we can't have during the fast, must be given to someone who is in need of it.

LOG-ON: DAY 12 – Morning Prayers

Enter these prayers with thanksgiving and adoration. Give the LORD worship this day. Now make these declarations and pray these points for five minutes as needed:

1. Under the covering of the Superior Blood of Jesus Christ, I decree an end to every operation of betrayal, financial hardship, emotional manipulation and interference in our church and departmental ministries.

2. Under the covering of the Superior Blood of Jesus, I deny the enemy access to our finances, property and opportunities for advancement through people on assignment, satanic operations, and points of contact.

3. Under the covering of the Superior Blood of Jesus, I release the blessings of the LORD to locate us in every circumstance, ministerial transaction, relationship and everyday activity in church.

4. Under the covering of the Superior Blood of Jesus Christ, I declare that goodness and mercy shall follow us all the days of our lives and we shall never depart from the House of our LORD.

5. Under the covering of the Superior Blood of Jesus Christ, I declare that any diverting spirit, personality, human vessel, satanic device or curse shall hereby cease operation in our finances, be permanently denied

access, be blinded and deafened to any of our movements and rendered mute. ALL missed opportunities, diverted wealth, lost investments, stolen money or goods shall be immediately returned SEVEN FOLD.

6. Under the covering of the Superior Blood of Jesus Christ, I decree that all monitoring spirits, devices, human vessels and points of contact be denied access to our lives, loved ones, finances and records. I declare that every monitoring spirit and vessel be blinded, desensitized and permanently displaced from every aspect of our lives.

7. Under the covering of the Superior Blood of Jesus Christ, I command that every satanic or soulish mark placed on us in the spirit, be washed away by the Blood of Jesus and that all our garments be changed to new, spotless, radiant garments fitted for our prophetic purposes.

8. Under the covering of the Superior Blood of Jesus Christ, I command divine order to be established in every dimension of our lives and the life of the church. I call for the spirit of good stewardship and excellence to be activated in our lives and in the lives of all church leaders and members.

9. Under the covering of the Superior Blood of Jesus Christ, I declare that all individual and corporate worship shall be offered to God in spirit and in truth. All individuals responsible for leading and assisting in praise and worship shall be empowered by the Holy Ghost in divine expression.

10. Under the covering of the Superior Blood of Jesus Christ, I declare that divine protection surrounds us and our loved ones as we travel over land, sea and by air. We are secured in the Blood of Jesus and nothing and no one can move us or provoke us to move ourselves (Psalm 121:3).

DAY 12
Sacrificial Giving

Is it not to deal thy bread to the hungry, and that thou bring the poor that are cast out to thy house? when thou seest the naked, that thou cover him; and that thou hide not thyself from thine own flesh?
Isaiah 58:7

WHEN YOU FAST, you become more compassionate for others who are hungry. Yahweh says the fast that I have chosen will concern those who are physically hungry.

God pronounces here the extremity of the Fasting that delights Him: "...and that thou hide not thyself from thine own flesh?" (Isaiah 58:7b)

There is a crucial demand here for an act of generosity that is extreme and costly. To understand this better, a careful examination of the above verse is imperative. The more literal modern versions agree with the KJV:

(ESV) "*and not to hide yourself from your **own flesh**?*"
(NASB) "*and not to hide yourself from your **own flesh**?*"
(NKJV) "*and not hide yourself from your **own flesh**?*"
(RSV) "*and not to hide yourself from your **own flesh**?*"

However, most other versions take an interpretative step, taking "flesh" to mean either family or all humankind. In other words, some interpret this to mean that God wants to extend this act of generosity to relatives or everyone we meet during the fasting.

Here is how the modern translations add to this fact:

(NLT) "*and do not hide from **relatives** who need your help.*"
(NIV) "*and not to turn away from your own **flesh and blood**?*"
(NET) "*Don't turn your back on your own **flesh and blood**!*"
(HCSB) "*and to not ignore your own **flesh and blood**?*"

I, however, do not believe that this is what is intended here in the scripture. These interpretations bypass all three of these important data:

- the progression of the verse (climactic parallelism)
- the point of the passage (giving of yourself to help the desperately needy)
- the most natural reading (giving even if it means facing need yourself).

To understand what is required here, let's look at the progression of the verse, for instance:

- to give bread
- to give shelter
- to give clothing.

Giving bread (meaning food) is the easiest of the three, you could say. Giving shelter is more dangerous, and most definitely not convenient. Giving clothing (keep in mind, we're talking about people in ancient times, not people with massive modern wardrobes) is a significant material sacrifice.

This is an example of "climactic parallelism," a device of Hebrew poetry which builds intensity. Though not a very common poetic device, climactic parallelism is nonetheless apparent in several places in Scripture and is recognized by scholars as one of the standard devices used by Hebrew poets.

The text builds here, from the easiest act of generosity required by God during our fast, to an inconvenient act of generosity, to a more significant personal sacrifice. So, to interpret this as, "oh be kind to your family" seems anticlimactic. This is not what God intends.

I believe that the text is using "flesh" (Hebrew: *basar*) in the normal, literal sense, not in the figurative sense. The figurative sense "relatives" is used in Scripture, but not nearly as much as the literal sense. So, "not hiding yourself from your own flesh" – means, to paraphrase: "Clothe the naked, even if it means you're giving him the very clothes off your own back!" For then, by missing the cloak you gave away to clothe a needy brother, you would not be "hiding yourself" from the sight of your own flesh. Generosity or charity is not only to be engaged in when we are enjoying prosperity; we are to give even if it seems as if such giving will place us in need.

What does all this mean? It simply means, Yahweh is calling us during this fasting season, to provide for the needs of others even if it means putting ourselves in need.

Whilst I believe this is what the text refers to here, mainstream thought, though, as reflected by many commentators and some translations, is that "flesh" here means "relatives." However, this translation never seems to be the product of intense deliberation, but assumed. Many commentaries glide over *basar*, focusing on the main point of the passage. I propose that *"basar"* is being used in a way very relevant to the main point.

Through study of church history and experientially in my own life, I know it's true: God will provide for you, even if your need is due to your over-abundant giving. And He provides so that we have more to give also. Devote this fasting season to give more even to the point of not having any left for yourself.

LOG-OFF: DAY 12 – Evening Prayers

Pray these prayers for five minutes each as necessary:

1. Under the covering of the Superior Blood of Jesus Christ, O God, forgive us for dedicating our lives and generations to becoming oracles of Satan. Have mercy upon us for we opened the door to spirits of divination and sorcery in our family lineage.
2. Under the covering of the Superior Blood of Jesus Christ, I repent and renounce any ancestral involvement in witchcraft, divination and occultism.
3. Under the covering of the Superior Blood of Jesus Christ, O Lord, by the blood of Jesus Christ, I separate myself from all the sins and the iniquities of my family lineage.
4. Under the covering of the Superior Blood of Jesus Christ, I renounce and reject all the practices of divination, witchcraft, sorcery, and idolatry, in the mighty name of Jesus.
5. Under the covering of the Superior Blood of Jesus Christ, all the negative records that are in the belly of the earth, in the waters and in the heavens which have given the devil a legal right to harass my destiny through sorcery, and divination, be consumed by the Holy Ghost fire.
6. Under the covering of the Superior Blood of Jesus Christ, I also nullify the negative pronouncements of such records upon my life and destiny, in the name of Jesus.
7. Under the covering of the Superior Blood of Jesus Christ, O Lord, help me to wrestle successfully against the wiles of the devil, in the name of Jesus.
8. Under the covering of the Superior Blood of Jesus Christ, I nullify every negative report ever made about me.

9. Under the covering of the Superior Blood of Christ, I cease to be a picture of failure. I cease to be abased, rejected, forsaken, desolate and downcast.
10. Under the covering of the Superior Blood of Jesus Christ, from today I will begin to manifest expressly every good thing God has written about me in His Book.

DAY 13
The Light of the World

Then shall thy light break forth as the morning, and thine health shall spring forth speedily: and thy righteousness shall go before thee; the glory of the LORD shall be thy rereward.
Isaiah 58:8

DAY 13 – The Light of the World

This is day thirteen of our fasting. We now progress into the blessings and rewards that accompanies God's chosen fast.

LOG-ON: DAY 13 – Morning Prayers

Enter these prayers with thanksgiving and adoration. Give the LORD worship this day. Now make these declarations and pray these points for 3 to 10 minutes as needed:

1. Under the covering of the Superior Blood of Jesus Christ, we declare that our children shall excel in their studies, sports and endeavors. They will be favored and advanced in every situation. They will not have dangerous accidents and they will grow up to accomplish their prophetic destiny with honor and distinction.

2. Under the covering of the Superior Blood of Jesus Christ, we declare that we will NOT die before our time. We will walk in health and strength all the days of our lives. We will joyfully accomplish everything God has assigned us to do with honor and distinction. We will enjoy blessings and the goodness of the LORD in the land of the living. We will serve the LORD all the days of our lives without offense (Psalm 118:17 and Psalm 91:16).

3. Under the covering of the Superior Blood of Jesus Christ, we declare that the territory of the church shall be enlarged with grace and ease. We call the hunters and fishermen of God to secure the right God-called workers for the right positions in the church. We release fresh revelation and THE

DISCIPLINE OF CONSISTENT PRAYER AND FASTING in the lives of every church member and leader (Jeremiah 16:16).

4. Under the covering of the Superior Blood of Jesus Christ, we command a renewed spirit of holiness, unity and boldness to overtake the church. We declare that the discernment of the leadership and members SHALL INCREASE DAILY and every false prophet and doctrine shall be exposed and thrown down.

5. Under the covering of the Superior Blood of Jesus Christ, we declare that the Blood of Jesus has wiped away all our sin guilt and the records of all our sins. We deploy the Blood of Jesus to locate and destroy every record of our sins and wrongdoing in hidden places, in the record books of Satan, in all satanic archives and in the memories of all demonic spirits and accomplices. In its place, a record of the innocent Blood of Jesus shall speak for us throughout eternity.

6. Under the covering of the Superior Blood of Jesus Christ, we deny all storms the power to distract us, to cause us to fear, or to speak fear in our lives. We decree that the peace of Jesus Christ is activated in every dimension of our lives and the lives of our loved ones.

7. Under the covering of the Superior Blood of Jesus Christ, in the name of Jesus, we revoke and negate every death wish, verdict and sentence of death in our lives, the lives of our loved ones, our children and in the lives of church leadership.

8. Under the covering of the Superior Blood of Jesus Christ, in the name of Jesus, we overthrow satanic sanctions and embargoes against us, our businesses, our loved ones, our children and church leadership. We exercise restraining orders over every strongman assigned to steal, kill and destroy us, our children, our loved ones and church leadership.

9. Under the covering of the Superior Blood of Jesus Christ, we intercept all satanic letters in circulation against us, our destinies and against the leadership of the church. We command that they be discontinued and brought to a permanent halt.

10. Under the covering of the Superior Blood of Jesus Christ, we decree a divine reversal of all satanic transactions that have taken place to devalue us and misrepresent our true selves.

DAY 13
The Light of the World

Then shall thy light break forth as the morning, and thine health shall spring forth speedily: and thy righteousness shall go before thee; the glory of the LORD shall be thy rereward.
Isaiah 58:8

YOU WANT TO MAKE SURE that you are doing the right thing. You are at a fork in the road and you do not know which way to go. Isaiah 58:8 says, *"Then your light shall break forth like the morning," It* is as if God turns on the lights and now you know what to do!

It's a picture of a long night being over. Have you ever had one of those long, dark nights where you wished and hoped for the dawn? God promises the "night" to be ripped apart and for the dawn to come.

As you fast and pray, God will light up your path. You will know you are in His will, and doing the right thing.

The word *light* means *"to shine"*. It also has the meaning of *"life and happiness"*. The word *morning* always means *"a new day"*. A new day will break forth in our lives when we fast the way God has set forth in His Word. Fasting illumines the soul so we can come into a proper relationship with the Spirit. Jesus was our example of the light. He revealed:

> *"As long as I am in the world, I am the light of the world"* – *John 9:5*

Jesus was the Light of the world as long as He was in the world. In His Sermon on the Mount, Jesus informed the people:

> *Ye are the light of the world. A city that is set on an hill cannot be hid.* – *Matthew 5:14*

The city set on the hill is the Mount Zion, the New Jerusalem that is coming down from Yahweh out of heaven prepared as a bride adorned for her husband (Revelation 21:2). Those who have sought Yahweh with their whole heart through fasting and prayer will make up that Holy City. Paul described these:

> *That ye may be blameless and harmless, the sons of God, without rebuke, in the midst of a crooked and perverse nation, among whom ye shine as lights in the world.* – *Philippians 2:15*

Yahweh will recognize those who are blameless (without blemish) and harmless (sincere) as sons. These will shine forth as His lights in the world in the midst of a crooked and perverse nation. As the world gets darker and the nations of the world become more crooked and perverse, the more the light of God's true church is going to shine forth.

Many will proclaim, "Jesus is still the light of the world". However, Yahweh is raising up His lights in the earth today to shine forth as the sun. In his second letter to the Thessalonians, Paul revealed:

> *Whereunto He called you by our gospel, to the obtaining of the glory of our Lord Jesus Christ."*
> *II Thessalonians 2:14*

Yahweh has called us to obtain the glory of our Lord Jesus Christ. As Paul wrote to the church at Corinth:

> *But we all, with open face beholding as in a glass the glory of the Lord, are changed into the same image from glory to glory, even as by the Spirit of the Lord. – II Corinthians 3:18*

We are to be changed from glory to glory until we come into the image of the Creator. This we can only do by and through the Spirit of the living God. Yahweh sent His Spirit on the Day of Pentecost to cleanse His creation from all unrighteousness. Only by and through the Spirit can we stand clean and pure before the Father of lights. We will be recreated into the same image and likeness of the Creator God as man was in the Garden before sin entered into man's existence.

Isaiah foretold this time when man through the anointing would again be adorned with the glory of God:

> *Arise, shine; for thy light is come, and the glory of the Lord is risen upon thee. – Isaiah 60:1*

How can we be assured that the glorious light of Yahweh will break forth in our lives? It will be when we overcome the old man through fasting, prayer and applying God's Word to our lives. When this process is complete, God's "new creation man" will spring forth in His image and likeness.

LOG-OFF: Day 13 - Evening Prayers

Confess, declare and pray along with these prayer-points for at least five minutes each:

1. Under the covering of the Blood of Jesus Christ, I dedicate and claim all our cities for Jesus, in Jesus' name.
2. Under the covering of the Blood of Jesus Christ, let the blessings and presence of the Lord be experienced in all our cities, in the name of Jesus.
3. Under the covering of the Blood of Jesus Christ, I decree total paralysis on lawlessness, immorality and drug-addiction in this country, in the name of Jesus.
4. Under the covering of the Blood of Jesus Christ, let the power, love and glory of God be established in our land, in the name of Jesus.
5. Under the covering of the Blood of Jesus Christ, Let there be thirst and hunger for God, in the hearts of Christians of this nation, in the name of Jesus.
6. Under the covering of the Blood of Jesus Christ, O Lord, deposit the spirit of revival in the United States of America (mention your own nation).
7. Under the covering of the Blood of Jesus Christ, O Lord, lay Your hands of power and might upon the Armed Forces and police, establishments and institutions, including universities and colleges of this country.
8. Under the covering of the Blood of Jesus Christ, let the resurrection power, of the Lord Jesus Christ fall upon our economy, in the name of Jesus.
9. Under the covering of the Blood of Jesus Christ, let there be fruitfulness and prosperity in every area of this country, in the name of Jesus.
10. Under the covering of the Blood of Jesus Christ, I command, every threat to the political, economic and social stability in the land to be paralyzed.

DAY 14
Fast Healing

Then shall thy light break forth as the morning, and thine health shall spring forth speedily: and thy righteousness shall go before thee; the glory of the LORD shall be thy rereward.
Isaiah 58:8

DAY 14 – Fast Healing

Correct fasting produces healing. As we continue with day fifteen of our fasting, continue to meditate on God's word and vigorously pray.

LOG-ON: Day 14 – Morning Prayers

Confess, declare and pray along with these prayer points for at least five minutes each:

1. Under the covering of the Blood of Jesus Christ, I frustrate every satanic external influence over our nation, in the name of Jesus.
2. Under the covering of the Blood of Jesus Christ, I command confusion and disagreement among the sons of the bondwoman planning to cage the nation, in Jesus' name.
3. Under the covering of the Blood of Jesus Christ, I break any covenant between any satanic external influence and our leaders, in the name of Jesus.
4. Under the covering of the Blood of Jesus Christ, I paralyze every spirit of wastage of economic resources in this country, in the name of Jesus.
5. Under the covering of the Blood of Jesus Christ, let the spirit of borrowing depart completely from this country, in the name of Jesus.
6. Under the covering of the Blood of Jesus Christ, O Lord, show Yourself mighty, in the affairs of this nation.
7. Under the covering of the Blood of Jesus Christ, let the kingdom of Christ come into this nation, in Jesus' name.
8. Under the covering of the Blood of Jesus Christ, O Lord, do new things in our country, to show Your power and greatness to the heathen.

9. Under the covering of the Blood of Jesus Christ, Let the kingdom of our Lord Jesus Christ come into the heart of every person in this country, in the name of Jesus.
10. Under the covering of the Blood of Jesus Christ, O Lord, have mercy upon this nation.

DAY 14

Fast Healing

Then shall thy light break forth as the morning, and thine health shall spring forth speedily: and thy righteousness shall go before thee; the glory of the LORD shall be thy rereward.
Isaiah 58:8

DO YOU HAVE A LOVED ONE who is in bad shape? Get serious and fast for them!

Is your health in question? Humble yourself before God and ask for healing. When there's no hope from a human perspective, put it in God's hands. He is the healer.

"*Your healing shall spring forth speedily...*" – Isaiah 58:8

Remember this is a promise that is attached to fasting and to prayer. The fast that I have chosen, says the Lord, is to meet your physical needs for healing.

Fasting is healthy. Many fast only for health reasons. Fasting cleanses the body of toxins and gives the body a chance to rest and be revitalized. God has promised when we fast our health will spring forth speedily; not only our physical health but also our Spiritual health.

Most do not realize our physical health has much to do with our Spiritual health. It becomes very difficult to worship and praise the Lord when we are sick. Even though we believe that God heals our physical illnesses, how can we ask Him to heal if we are violating His directives (His written Word)?

Many suffer illness because they have violated God's Word, by refusing to act on His promises. Just as it is very difficult to worship and praise the Lord when we are sick, it becomes much more difficult to seek the Lord when physical illness hinders us. God has given us fasting that we may seek the Lord with our whole heart; our total thinking process. God promised Israel:

> *"If from thence thou shalt seek the Lord thy God, thou shalt find Him, if thou seek Him with all thy heart and with all thy soul." – Deuteronomy 4:29*

Those who seek Yahweh with all their hearts and souls shall find Him. It is not that God is lost, but in our seeking Him our Spiritual health will spring forth speedily. When we are healthy, both physically and Spiritually, we will know the will of Yahweh in our Lives and do it. God has promised fasting will improve our relationship with Him.

When speaking to His disciples, Jesus disclosed:

> *"And I say unto you, Ask, and it shall be given you; seek, and ye shall find; knock, and it shall be opened unto you. For every*

> *one that asketh receiveth; and he that seeketh findeth; and to him that knocketh it shall be opened."* – Luke 11:9-10

We may ask the question, "How do we ask? How do we seek? How do we knock?" Many times, Scriptures simply become platitudes. We mouth the Word and never seek the meaning.

The word **ask** means *"to present your petition"*.

The word **seek** means *"to inquire, to covet earnestly, striving to obtain"*.

The word **knock** means *"to get one's attention"*.

When we fast, we come into a position to present our petitions because we earnestly covet God's attention. We have God's promise that if we ask, seek, and knock we will receive our petition from Him.

Many whose relationship with God is spiritually sick need to begin to act on the promises of Yahweh. When we do, His Spiritual healing will truly spring forth speedily.

LOG-OFF: Day 14 – Evening Prayers

Confess, declare and pray along with these prayer points for at least five minutes each:

1. Under the covering of the Blood of Jesus Christ, let all the glory of this nation that has departed be restored, in the name of Jesus.
2. Under the covering of the Blood of Jesus Christ, let all un-evangelized areas of this country be reached with the Gospel of our Lord Jesus Christ, in the name of Jesus.
3. Under the covering of the Blood of Jesus Christ, O Lord, send forth laborers into Your vineyard, to reach the unreached in this country.
4. Under the covering of the Blood of Jesus Christ, I dismantle, the stronghold of poverty in this nation, in the name of Jesus.
5. Under the covering of the Blood of Jesus Christ, O Lord, install Your agenda for this nation.
6. Under the covering of the Blood of Jesus Christ, let every power of darkness operating in our educational institutions be disgraced, in the name of Jesus.
7. Under the covering of the Blood of Jesus Christ, let the satanic representatives of key posts in this country, be dismantled, in the name of Jesus.
8. Under the covering of the Blood of Jesus Christ, let every evil spiritual throne behind all physical thrones in the United States of America (put the name of your own country), be dismantled, in the name of Jesus.
9. Under the covering of the Blood of Jesus Christ, let every satanic covenant made on behalf of this country by anyone, be nullified, in the name of Jesus.
10. Under the covering of the Blood of Jesus Christ, I trample upon the serpents and scorpions of ethnic or racial clashes in this country, in the name of Jesus.

Day 15
The Gift of Righteousness

*Then shall thy light break forth as the morning, and thine health shall spring forth speedily: and **thy righteousness shall go before thee**; the glory of the LORD shall be thy rereward.*
Isaiah 58:8

Day 15 – The Gift of Righteousness

As you walk with the Lord, you will gain a reputation as a person who does the right thing.

LOG-ON: DAY 15 – Morning Prayers

Pray these prayers for yourself, family, and the nation you dwell in that God will show mercy and over-turn His wrath and judgment. Stay on each prayer point for at least fives minutes as necessary:

1. Under the covering of the Blood of Jesus Christ, Father, in the name of Jesus, I confess all the sins and iniquities of the land, of our ancestors, of our leaders, and of the people; for example, violence, rejection of God, corruption, idolatry, robbery, suspicion, injustice, bitterness, bloody riots, pogroms, rebellion, conspiracy, shedding of innocent blood, racial discrimination, child-kidnapping and murder, occultism, mismanagement, negligence, etcetera.
2. Under the covering of the Blood of Jesus Christ, I plead for mercy and forgiveness, in the name of Jesus.
3. Under the covering of the Blood of Jesus Christ, O Lord, remember our land and redeem it.
4. Under the covering of the Blood of Jesus Christ, O Lord, save our land from destruction and judgment.
5. Under the covering of the Blood of Jesus Christ, let Your healing power begin to operate upon our land, in Jesus' name.
6. Under the covering of the Blood of Jesus Christ, let all forces of darkness, hindering the move of God in this nation be rendered impotent, in the name of Jesus.

7. Under the covering of the Blood of Jesus Christ, I command the spiritual strongman in charge of this country, to be bound and be disgraced, in the name of Jesus.
8. Under the covering of the Blood of Jesus Christ, let every evil establishment and satanic tree in this country be uprooted and cast into fire, in the name of Jesus.
9. Under the covering of the Blood of Jesus Christ, I come against every spirit of the anti-Christ working against this nation and I command them to be permanently frustrated, in the name of Jesus.
10. Under the covering of the Blood of Jesus Christ, I command the stones of fire from God to fall upon every national satanic operation and activity, in Jesus' name.

DAY 15

The Gift of Righteousness

*Then shall thy light break forth as the morning, and thine health shall spring forth speedily: and **thy righteousness shall go before thee**; the glory of the LORD shall be thy rereward.*
Isaiah 58:8

A PERSON IN RIGHT STANDING with GOD cannot fail on their knees. The battle is in your favor, if you are standing rightly with Yahweh.

> *"But of Him are ye in Christ Jesus, who of God is made unto us wisdom, and righteousness, and sanctification, and redemption:"*
> – I Corinthians 1:30

In ourselves we have no righteousness. Christ Jesus is our righteousness. As Isaiah the prophet wrote:

> *But we are all as an unclean thing, and all our righteousnesses are as filthy rags: and we all do fade as a leaf; and our iniquities like the wind, have taken us away. – Isaiah 64:6*

Many believe they are righteous because they act righteous. But our own righteousness is as filthy rags before God. The Apostle Paul revealed to the church at Rome:

> *For if by one man's offence death reigned by one; much more they which receive abundance of grace and of the gift of righteousness shall reign in life by one, Jesus Christ.– Romans 5:17*

Righteousness is a Spiritual gift. Only those who dwell, walk, and live in the Spirit can obtain the gift of righteousness. James wrote:

> *And the fruit of righteousness is sown in peace of them that make peace. – James 3:18*

Righteousness is a fruit of the Spirit. Paul also wrote to the church at Corinth:

> *Awake to righteousness, and sin not; for some have not the knowledge of God. I speak this to your shame.– I Corinthians 15:34*

Paul advised us to awake to righteousness and sin not. Many are still dwelling in their Adamic sleep. Their Spiritual eyes are closed to the ways and the will of God. They have become part of a religious system that says you are all right with God as long as you attend here and do as we say. Paul addresses those who are being held in bondage to their spirit of religion:

> *For they being ignorant of God's righteousness, and going about to establish their own righteousness, have not submitted themselves unto the righteousness of God. - Romans 10:3*

The righteousness of God does not go before those who are ignorant of His righteousness. Those ignorant of God's righteousness are still trying to obtain and establish their own righteousness. They create their own moral code to live by based on their errant, religious doctrine. God has given us the way to obtain true righteousness by and through fasting. In his second letter to the Corinthians, Paul wrote:

> *For He hath made Him to be sin for us, who knew no sin; that we might be made the righteousness of God in Him.– II Corinthians 5:21*

Jesus came to be made sin for us that we may once again be made the righteousness of God. This does not come automatically when we come into His saving grace. It must be sought with our whole hearts, souls and spirits. God must be our whole desire if we are to have His righteousness go before us. Paul spoke of the new man we will become if we seek God with our whole hearts:

> *And that ye put on the new man, which after God is created in righteousness and true holiness. Ephesians 4:24*

Our new man is created in God's righteousness and His true holiness. Until we are recreated in righteousness and true holiness, we will never dwell in the presence of God. Jesus gave us directions on how we may stand again in His presence:

> *But seek ye first the Kingdom of God, and His righteousness; and all these things shall be added unto you.– Matthew 6:33*

We must first seek the Kingdom of God. Along with this we must seek the righteousness of God. Then all that God has for us will be added unto us. The question is, "How do we seek God's Kingdom and His righteousness? The answer is through fasting. God has promised that if we fast, His righteousness will go before us.

LOG-OFF: DAY 15 – Evening Prayers

Pray these prayers for yourself, family and the nation you dwell in that God will show mercy and overturn his wrath and judgment. Stay on each prayer point for at least five minutes as necessary:

1. Under the covering of the Blood of Jesus Christ, let the desires, plans, devices and expectations of the enemy for this country, be completely frustrated, in Jesus' name.
2. Under the covering of the Blood of Jesus Christ, let every satanic curse on this nation, fall down to the ground and die, in the name of Jesus.
3. Under the covering of the Blood of Jesus Christ, by the blood of Jesus, let all sins, ungodliness, idolatry and vices cease in the land, in the name of Jesus.
4. Under the covering of the Blood of Jesus Christ, I break every evil covenant and dedication made upon our land, in the name of Jesus.
5. Under the covering of the Blood of Jesus Christ, I plead the blood of Jesus, over the nation.
6. Under the covering of the Blood of Jesus Christ, I decree the will of God for this land, whether the devil likes it or not, in the name of Jesus.
7. Under the covering of the Blood of Jesus Christ, let all contrary powers and authorities in the United States of America (mention your own nation here), be confounded and be put to shame.
8. Under the covering of the Blood of Jesus Christ, I close every satanic gate in every city of this country.
9. Under the covering of the Blood of Jesus Christ, let every evil throne in this country be dashed to pieces, in Jesus' name.
10. Under the covering of the Superior Blood of Jesus Christ, I bind all negative forces, operating in the lives of the leaders of this country, in the name of Jesus.

Day 16
God's Got Your Back

*Then shall thy light break forth as the morning, and thine health shall spring forth speedily: and thy righteousness shall go before thee; **the glory of the LORD shall be thy rereward.***
Isaiah 58:8

Day 16 – God's Got Your Back

Correct fasting is all about moving ahead. It is not just about looking back and mourning over sins, but when there is mourning involved, it's about putting the past behind and moving ahead. Fasting helps you move forward.

LOG-OFF: DAY 16 – Morning Prayers

Pray these prayers for five minutes each as necessary:

1. Under the covering of the Superior Blood of Jesus Christ, Heavenly Father, I come before You, through Your Son Jesus Christ who died for me on the cross.
2. Under the covering of the Superior Blood of Jesus Christ, I thank You Lord that Jesus took away all of my sins and iniquities when He was crucified.
3. Under the covering of the Superior Blood of Jesus Christ, today, I acknowledge all the sins of idolatry, ancestral worship, divination, and witchcraft that we and our forefathers committed before You.
4. Under the covering of the Superior Blood of Jesus Christ, Father, we have sinned before You. Forgive us from seeking knowledge through demonic mediums and satanic priests.
5. Under the covering of the Superior Blood of Jesus Christ, we repent from the sins of seeking guidance through familiar spirits, spirits of the dead, necromancy, horoscopes, witchdoctors, mediums, false prophets, and calling psychics.
6. Under the covering of the Superior Blood of Jesus Christ, O Lord, forgive us and be merciful upon us. Heavenly Father, forgive us also where we have murdered people through witchcraft practices and sorcery.
7. Under the Covering of the Superior Blood of Jesus Christ, let Your mercy be upon us and forgive us, in the name of Jesus.

8. Under the covering of the Superior Blood of Jesus Christ, O God, I confess and repent from all the incantations, enchantments we have made against the success and progress of others.
9. Under the covering of the Superior Blood of Jesus Christ, Heavenly Father, I also confess the sins of murder and bloodshed. In any way we have murdered or killed human beings, forgive us, in the name of Jesus.
10. Under the covering of the Superior Blood of Jesus Christ, O God, I bring repentance for the sin of raising up a satanic priesthood in our family lineage. I confess that we and our forefathers have dishonored You and rejected Your holy ordinances.

DAY 16
God's Got Your Back

Then shall thy light break forth as the morning, and thine health shall spring forth speedily: and thy righteousness shall go before thee; **the glory of the LORD shall be thy rereward.**
Isaiah 58:8

GOD'S GLORY WILL BE YOUR "rear guard". I don't want to go too deeply into this but let's just put it in modern vernacular: God's got your back.

When do you need a "rear guard"?
You need a "rear guard" when you are looking and moving forward. When you fast and serve the Lord in God's manner, you don't need to keep looking over your shoulder

wondering what's going to bite you from behind. God's got your back.

The word **rereward** means *"to gather, to collect, to assemble or to take in"*. When we fast, God has promised to release His glory in our lives. The word rereward was used to denote the harvest time in Israel, the time of ingathering. This feast took place at the end of their agricultural year. This feast was called the Feast of Ingathering.

The Feast of Ingathering was also called the Feast of Tabernacles. This was when all Israel came together to dwell in temporary dwelling places. All Israel's feasts have been fulfilled in prophecy except the Feast of Tabernacles. God is about to institute His Feast of Ingathering. When He brings in His harvest, those who are mature, complete, and whole will be part of this ingathering process. The prophet Isaiah spoke of this time of ingathering:

> *For ye shall not go out with haste, nor go by flight: for the Lord will go before you; and the God of Israel will be your rereward. – Isaiah 52:12*

We will not go out with haste, nor by flight. Some believe they are simply going to fly away. In this misconception, there is no overcoming, no change, and no seeking of God needed. God is warning His people to prepare themselves because the Kingdom of God is at hand. Through fasting we can hear God's direction for these last days.

The time of harvest is upon the earth. God's righteousness will go before us and His glory will be our rereward. He will gather His people unto Himself. Jesus stated:

> *But go rather to the lost sheep of the house of Israel"– Matthew 10:6*

Jesus' first coming was to the lost sheep of the house of Israel. When He was about to enter Jerusalem, knowing He would be crucified, Jesus wept over Jerusalem. He did not weep for Himself, not for what He would suffer, but for the people. He stated:

> *O Jerusalem, Jerusalem, thou that killest the prophets, and stonest them which are sent unto thee, how often would I have gathered thy children together, even as a hen gathereth her chickens under her wings, and ye would not! – Matthew 23:37*

Jesus wanted to gather His people unto Himself at that time, but they would not heed. God is desiring to gather His people unto Himself today, but the same is true. They will not seek Him in fasting and prayer. Because of this, God's glory has been withheld and those who are not prepared will not be part of His Feast of Tabernacles; the time of ingathering. They will not be part of what Paul revealed to the church at Thessalonica:

> *When He shall come to be glorified in His saints, and to be admired in all them that believe because our testimony among you was believed in that day. – II Thessalonians 1:10*

God is coming to be glorified in His saints; those who have entered in through the fast that God has ordained. Those who have sought God with their whole hearts shall be gathered together in the glory of God.

We fast because there is a divine reward in fasting. Yahweh honors a heart that is supplicated and surrendered to Him. Fasting humbles us, breaks the power of sin, and allows the Holy Spirit to perfect God's work in us. Yahweh intervenes when His people rise up in fasting and prayer. Lets read Isaiah 58: 8-9:

> *Then shall thy light break forth as the morning, and thine health shall spring forth speedily: and thy*

righteousness shall go before thee; the glory of the LORD shall be thy reward.

Then shalt thou call, and the LORD shall answer; thou shalt cry, and he shall say, Here I am. If thou take away from the midst of thee the yoke, the putting forth of the finger, and speaking vanity.

⇒ TIPS FOR TODAY

God's Blessing (vv. 8-9)

- Your light will break forth: You shall receive the magnetizing favor of God to shine where you have once been resisted. You shall be honored and lifted amongst many.
- Your health will spring forth: Miraculous healings and divine restoration will take place in your body, soul and spirit. Expect this move of God in your life as you partake in this fasting.
- Your righteousness will go before you: Hold your peace, in whatever situation or trouble you find yourself entangled, the LORD will speak in your favor during or after this fasting.
- The Glory of the LORD shall be your rearward: As David has said, the LORD will comfort you on all sides. He will shield us in His eternal Glory; hidden from all snares and wiles of the wicked one. His Glory shall be our covering; hence, you shall be seen differently.

PRAYER GUIDE 16:
- Pray that the LORD will cause your light to break forth.

- Pray for the uncommon favor of God to affect your lifestyle and environment.
- Pray for divine elevation and divine enablement to function.
- Pray that your body, soul and spirit will receive divine health and restoration.
- Pray that the LORD will cause your righteousness to go before you this year.
- Pray that the Glory of the LORD God shall be your rearward and security for the entire year.
- Pray that the LORD God will shield you in His glory and hide you from all snares and wiles of the wicked one.

LOG-OFF: DAY 16 – Evening Prayers

Pray these prayers for yourself, your family, and the nation you dwell in that God will show mercy and overturn his wrath and judgment. Stay on each prayer point for at least five minutes as necessary:

1. Under the covering of the Blood of Jesus Christ, O Lord, lay Your hands of fire and power upon all our leaders, in the name of Jesus.
2. Under the covering of the Blood of Jesus Christ, let the mercy of God fall upon this country, in Jesus' name.
3. Under the covering of the Blood of Jesus Christ, let the Prince of Peace, reign in every department of this nation, in the name of Jesus.
4. Under the covering of the Blood of Jesus Christ, let every anti-gospel spirit, be frustrated and be rendered impotent, in the name of Jesus.
5. Under the covering of the Blood of Jesus Christ, O Lord, give us leaders who will see their roles as a calling, instead of an opportunity to amass wealth.
6. Under the covering of the Blood of Jesus Christ, let all forms of ungodliness be destroyed, by the divine fire of burning, in the name of Jesus.
7. Under the covering of the Blood of Jesus Christ, O Lord, let our leaders be filled with divine understanding and wisdom.
8. Under the covering of the Blood of Jesus Christ, O Lord, let our leaders follow the counsel of God and not of man and demons.
9. Under the covering of the Blood of Jesus Christ, O Lord, let our leaders have wisdom and knowledge of God.
10. Under the covering of the Blood of Jesus Christ, O Lord, let our government be the kind that would obtain Your direction and leading.

Day 17

Power Through Fasting

Then shalt thou call, and the LORD shall answer; thou shalt cry, and he shall say, Here I am. If thou take away from the midst of thee the yoke, the putting forth of the finger, and speaking vanity
Isaiah 58:9

Day 17 – Power Through Fasting

The fast that I have chosen, God says, will bring you the answer you have been needing.

LOG-ON: DAY 17 – Morning Prayers

Enter these prayers with thanksgiving and adoration. Give the LORD worship this day. Now make these declarations and pray these points for five minutes each as needed:

Confessions: Make these confessions to establish your identity in Christ Jesus:

1. Under the covering of the Blood of Jesus Christ, the Bible says because I believe and receive Jesus Christ, power has been given to me to become a son of God, and I am empowered to trample upon serpents and scorpions and all the powers of the enemy.
2. Under the covering of the Blood of Jesus Christ, I am empowered to use the name of Jesus to cast out demons and heal the sick.
3. Under the covering of the Blood of Jesus Christ, I am empowered to bind, to loose and to decree things and the Bible says wherever my voice is heard no one can ask me why.
4. Under the covering of the Blood of Jesus Christ, I do these things for my voice is the voice of a king that is full of authority.
5. Under the covering of the Blood of Jesus Christ, I am commanded and empowered by my God to subdue and to exercise dominion. For I am made a little lower than the angels and God has crowned me

with glory and honor and has also made me to have dominion over all the works of His hands.

6. Under the covering of the Blood of Jesus Christ, the devil that was against my authority as God's representative on earth has been destroyed by Christ. The keys of the kingdom of heaven are given to me and because I am a member of the body of Christ, which is the Church, the gates of hell cannot prevail against me.

7. Under the covering of the Blood of Jesus Christ, because the grace of God is upon my life as the light of His glory, I am full of divine favor. I am a partaker of all of heaven's spiritual blessings.

8. Under the covering of the Blood of Jesus Christ, I am an overcomer; the Bible says whosoever is born of God overcomes the world, and this is the victory that overcomes the world, even my faith.

9. Under the covering of the Blood of Jesus Christ, in faith I overcome ungodly worry, anxiety, heaviness of spirit, sorrow, depression, lust of the eyes and lust of the flesh.

10. Under the covering of the Blood of Jesus Christ, in faith I have overcome all the tricks of the devil, for it is written, greater is Jesus Christ who dwells in me than the devil that is in the world.

DAY 17

Power Through Destiny

Then shalt thou call, and the LORD shall answer; thou shalt cry, and he shall say, Here I am. If thou take away from the midst of thee the yoke, the putting forth of the finger, and speaking vanity
Isaiah 58:9

EFFECTIVE PRAYER IS SUPPOSED to be one of the primary purposes of fasting. Do you want God to answer your prayers? Consider fasting.

You shall call and the Lord shall answer

God informed the people they were not to fast to make their voices heard on high, or to try to force Him to hear their petitions. God has promised if our fast is acceptable in His sight, when we call upon Him, He will answer speedily.

When we fast to come into God's will, it is then that we can claim all His promises. Peter revealed:

> *The Lord is not slack concerning His promises as some men count slackness – II Peter 3:9*

We can depend on God's wonderful promises. The prophet Isaiah penned God's words:

> *And it shall come to pass, that before they call, I will answer; and while they are yet speaking, I will hear. – Isaiah 65:24*

When we enter into a fast it should be for the primary purpose of hearing from the Lord and seeking His will. Isaiah spoke that before we call God would answer, and when we speak, He would hear. The beloved John wrote:

> *This is the confidence that we have in Him, that, if we ask any thing according to His will, He heareth us: – I John 5:14*

When we fast and seek God's will, then He hears us and answers our prayers. Fasting enhances our prayer life. Fasting gets the old man, the carnal nature out of the way so God's voice can be heard. Isaiah related:

> *And thine ears shall hear a word behind thee, saying, This is the way, walk ye in it, when ye turn to the right hand, and when ye turn to the left. – Isaiah 30:21*

When we cease from our labors and come totally away to hear the voice of God through fasting, then His still, small voice can be heard. Many will say, "God doesn't speak to me". He may be speaking, but perhaps you are not in the place where you can hear. Perhaps the noise of the life you are living is drowning out His still, small voice in your life. It is God's desire that we hear Him. In Jesus' words:

> *And when He putteth forth His own sheep, He goeth before them, and the sheep follow Him: for they know His voice. – John 10:4*

Through fasting, God's sheep will come to the place where they will hear His voice and follow Him. They will come to the place in their walk that when they call to God, they will hear Him say, *"Here I am"*, Isaiah 58:9.

The prophet Zechariah spoke of those who would enter into God's glory. He wrote:

> *For thus saith the Lord of hosts; After the glory hath He sent me unto the nations which spoiled you: for he that toucheth you toucheth the apple of His eye. – Zechariah 2:8*

He that toucheth you toucheth the apple of God's eye, or those who have come into the center of God's attention. God has made all these wonderful promises to those who fast in His will. That is not the end of God's promise, He proclaimed:

> *If thou take away from the midst of thee the yoke, the putting forth of the finger and speaking vanity. Isaiah 58:9b*

God lists three things that must be removed from our lives if we are to receive His promises.

1. We must put off the yoke
   - If we are holding anyone in bondage it must cease. If anyone is holding us in bondage, it must be broken.
2. We must stop pointing the finger
   - This is an accusing act. We must cease from accusing our brothers and sisters in Christ.
3. We must cease from speaking vanity

- The word **vanity** means "*nothingness, worthlessness, of no value*". Jesus referred to these as "idle words":

> *But I say unto you, That every idle word that men shall speak, they shall give account thereof in the day of judgment. – Matthew 12:36*

Those who speak vanity will give an account before God on the Day of Judgment. Isaiah continued:

> *And if thou draw out thy soul to the hungry, and satisfy the afflicted soul; then shall thy light rise in obscurity, and thy darkness be as the noonday: – Isaiah 58:10*

God's people are more in need of Spiritual food than they are physical food. When we draw out our soul to meet their Spiritual needs and satisfy their afflicted souls, our light will arise, and that which was hidden in darkness in our lives will be as the noonday.

> *And the Lord shall guide thee continually, and satisfy thy soul in drought, and make fat thy bones: and thou shalt be like a watered garden, and like a spring of water, whose waters fail not. And they that shall be of thee shall build the old waste places: thou shalt raise up the foundations of many generations; and thou shalt be called, The repairer of the breach, The Restorer of paths to dwell in.- Isaiah 58:11-12*

God has promised to be our continual guide, to satisfy our parched dry soul, and to make our lives prosperous in the things of God. Our lives will be as a watered garden and our water (the active Word of God in our lives) will never fail. As Jesus spoke to the woman at the well:

> *But whosoever drinketh of the water that I shall give Him shall never thirst; but the water that I shall give Him shall be in Him a well of water springing up into everlasting life. John 4:14*

When we drink from the wells of living water, the water that will never fail, then that water will spring up in us and produce everlasting life. Through the pen of Isaiah God promised that those whose fast is acceptable in His sight will be the Repairers of the Breach. We will repair the breach that came between God and His creation because of sin. Those who keep God's acceptable fast will restore the paths that God has intended for His creation to walk in.

To the church at Corinth, Paul reveals the depth of God's promises:

> *For all the promises of God in Him are yea, and in Him Amen, unto the glory of God by us. - II Corinthians 1:20*

God never draws back from His promise. Failure only comes when man falls short of meeting the conditions to receive them. God has given us fasting for a particular purpose and that is to seek His will and His way. Fasting brings us into a place where God can communicate with us. We must be willing to afflict the flesh so that the Spirit may be released to do the will of God.

LOG-OFF: Evening Prayers

Make this confession boldly:

You are my Lord and my God. I know from Your Word that a broken spirit, a broken and a contrite heart is a sacrifice, O God, that You will not despise.
I come before you now to offer myself to you Lord God – all of me – my body, my mind and my soul. All I have, all I am, are Yours and Yours alone.
O Lord God, as I submit myself to you, I commit to doing everything I do, to saying everything I say, and to choosing everything I choose, for the sake of Your Kingdom and not mine.

Stand on these prayer points for five minutes each as necessary to pray:

1. Under the covering of the Blood of Jesus Christ, I commit my works to Him and my thoughts are established.
2. Under the covering of the Blood of Jesus Christ, I do not take God for granted for before I do anything or go anywhere, I acknowledge Him so as to walk by divine direction.
3. Under the covering of the Blood of Jesus Christ, I am committed to an obedience lifestyle.
4. Under the covering of the Blood of Jesus Christ, I can do all things through Christ that strengthens me.
5. Under the covering of the Blood of Jesus Christ, I am committed to a life of excellence.
6. Under the covering of the Blood of Jesus Christ, I am not reserving any part of myself, my possessions,

my energy and time from you because I am now aware of the plan that you have for me and I am willing to do what you expect of me.
7. Under the covering of the Blood of Jesus Christ, I know that if I make less than 100-percent surrender to you, the devil will take advantage of any space I leave to make inroad into that uncommitted area of my life.
8. Under the covering of the Blood of Jesus Christ, I am totally surrendered to the Father of spirits. He is my all in all.
9. Under the covering of the Blood of Jesus Christ, I am willing to place my trust in the wisdom and the will of God.
10. Under the covering of the Blood of Jesus Christ, Lord I thank you for the commitment I have to help members of my physical and spiritual families.

DAY 18

The Heart of the Fast

Then shalt thou call, and the LORD *shall answer; thou shalt cry, and he shall say, Here I am. If thou take away from the midst of thee the yoke, the putting forth of the finger, and speaking vanity; And if thou draw out thy soul to the hungry, and satisfy the afflicted soul; then shall thy light rise in obscurity, and thy darkness be as the noon day.*
Isaiah 58:9-10 -

DAY 18 – The Heart of The Fast

Praise God! It's the eighteenth day of our one month fasting and prayer. It has been a long journey so far. Pray for divine enablement and strength to continue the rest of the fasting period.

LOG-ON: DAY 18 – Morning Prayers

Pray these prayers for yourself, your family, and the nation you dwell in, that God will show mercy and overturn His wrath and judgment. Stay on each prayer point for five minutes each as necessary:

1. Under the covering of the Blood of Jesus Christ, let every satanic altar in this country receive the fire of God and be burned to ashes, in the name of Jesus.
2. Under the covering of the Blood of Jesus Christ, I silence every satanic prophet, priest and practitioner, in the mighty name of Jesus. I forbid them from interfering with the affairs of this nation, in the name of Jesus.
3. Under the covering of the Blood of Jesus Christ, let the blood of Jesus, cleanse our land from every blood pollution, in the name of Jesus.
4. Under the covering of the Blood of Jesus Christ, I command the fire of God on all idols, sacrifices, rituals, shrines and local satanic thrones in this country, in Jesus' name.
5. Under the covering of the Blood of Jesus Christ, I break any conscious and unconscious agreement made between the people of this country and Satan, in Jesus' name.
6. Under the covering of the Blood of Jesus Christ, I boldly confess that my great commission has come, my change has come, my transformation is here, my lifting has come, new things are happening in my life. This is my time and my season, I shall never remain the same again in Jesus' name. Amen.

7. Under the covering of the Blood of Jesus Christ, my heart is yielded to do the will of God. His love fills my heart.
8. Under the covering of the Blood of Jesus Christ, I am anointed to operate in holy zeal.
9. Under the covering of the Blood of Jesus Christ, I boldly declare that the grace of God will help me to be faithful to the end, and to walk in righteousness all the days of my life.
10. Under the covering of the Superior Blood of Jesus Christ, from today I will begin to manifest expressly every good thing God has written about me in His Book.

Day 18

Th Heart of The Fast

Then shalt thou call, and the LORD shall answer; thou shalt cry, and he shall say, Here I am. If thou take away from the midst of thee the yoke, the putting forth of the finger, and speaking vanity; And if thou draw out thy soul to the hungry, and satisfy the afflicted soul; then shall thy light rise in obscurity, and thy darkness be as the noonday.
Isaiah 58:9-10 -

GOD HAS PROMISED during this fast, that if you will forgive others and loose the bondages of wickedness done against you, your prayer shall be answered. By releasing others who have hurt you, you have opened the channel for answered prayers, for God to intervene, and for Him to act in your life.

It is clear what God wants from us, in order to answer our prayers:

In order to answer our prayers, God wants us to cease from our wicked ways and sinful nature. (vv. 9b -10a)

- Do not quarrel with anyone or speak evil of anyone.
- Avoid gossips and false advisement of other people's lifestyles.
- Do not be anyone's burden or grieve anyone unbearably.
- Put away the finger pointing, insults, profanity, and anything unbecoming of a Christian.
- If it depends on you, live at peace with all people.
- Examine yourself wholly as you present yourself to the LORD in prayer. If you have wronged anyone, call him or her. At best see him or her and apologize.
- Be sincere and genuine. Forgive and you shall be forgiven.

PRAYER GUIDE 18:

- Pray that the Spirit of God will lead you to settle any quarrel with anyone.
- Pray that you'll let go of any grudge and animosity against follow believers.
- Pray that the Spirit of God will guide your tongue, and you will not gossip, use profane language or speak evil against anyone.
- Pray for patience and the combined fruit of the Spirit recorded in Galatians 5:22.
- Pray for each of the fruit of the Spirit until its qualities manifest within you.
- Pray against the works of the flesh recorded in Galatians 5:19-21 operating in our members.
- Pray against each of the problems recorded in Galatians 5:19-21 until you're totally delivered.

LOG-OFF: Day 18 - Evening Prayer

Spend time to make these confessions and declarations over your life. You may pray each prayer point for five minutes each if needed:

1. Under the covering of the Blood of Jesus Christ, Lord, give me the gifts of the Holy Spirit by your Spirit and His fruits to manifest in my life in Jesus' name.
2. Under the covering of the Blood of Jesus Christ, Father, I ask that you endow me with the gift of the Holy Spirit in Jesus' name.
3. Under the covering of the Blood of Jesus Christ, Father let there be manifestation and demonstration of the gifts of the Spirit in my life to profit my generation.
4. Under the covering of the Blood of Jesus Christ, Father, cause me to manifest your power and your authority by the Holy Spirit and cause me to be terror to the kingdom of darkness in Jesus' name.
5. Under the covering of the Blood of Jesus Christ, Father, cause me to cast out devils and heal all manner of diseases by the power of the Holy Spirit upon me in Jesus' name.
6. Under the covering of the Blood of Jesus Christ, Lord, as you endow me with the gift of the Spirit, help me not to be proud, in Jesus' name.
7. Under the covering of the Blood of Jesus Christ, Father grant me divine wisdom as you gave Solomon.
8. Under the covering of the Blood of Jesus Christ, Father, give me wisdom to fear you and to obey your commandments in Jesus' name.

9. Under the covering of the Blood of Jesus Christ, Lord, give me wisdom that will make my ways prosperous in Jesus' name.
10. Under the covering of the Blood of Jesus Christ, Father, as wisdom is the principal thing, grant me divine wisdom from above to know what to do in times of decision in Jesus' name.

DAY 19
The Breaking Point

Then shall thy light break forth as the morning, and thine health shall spring forth speedily: and thy righteousness shall go before thee; the glory of the Lord shall be thy reward. Then shalt thou call, and the Lord shall answer; thou shalt cry, and he shall say, Here I am. If thou take away from the midst of thee the yoke, the putting forth of the finger, and speaking vanity
-Isaiah 58:8-9

DAY 19 – The Breaking Point

This is Day 19, and by now your experience with God is under-going a remarkable transformation. If you haven't gotten there yet, don't worry. There is something prepared for all of us if we do this right.

LOG-ON: DAY 19 – Morning Prayers

Enter these prayers with thanksgiving and adoration. Give the LORD worship this day. Now make these declarations and pray these points for 3 to 10 minutes as needed:

Confessions: Make these confessions to establish your identity in Christ Jesus:

1. Under the covering of the Blood of Jesus Christ, no weapon that is formed against me shall prosper.
2. Under the covering of the Blood of Jesus Christ, in righteousness I am established; I am far from oppression, for I shall not fear, and from terror for it shall not come near me.
3. Under the covering of the Blood of Jesus Christ, the Lord shall cover me with His feathers, because I have made Him my dwelling place.
4. Under the covering of the Blood of Jesus Christ, evil shall not befall me; I shall tread upon the lion and the cobra and surely the Lord will always deliver me from the snare of the fowlers. God has made me a beneficiary of divine health through the stripes that were laid on Jesus Christ.
5. Under the covering of the Blood of Jesus Christ, through Jesus Christ I have access to the throne of grace of God, to find peace with God.

6. Under the covering of the Blood of Jesus Christ, I have prosperity, for God will no longer withhold any good thing from me.

7. Under the covering of the Blood of Jesus Christ, I have spoken with the tongue of the learned and as it is written, I shall be justified by the words of my mouth.

8. Under the covering of the Blood of Jesus Christ, I ask that the Word of God I have confessed, begin to transform me to the original image God designed me to be in His book.

9. Under the covering of the Blood of Jesus Christ, I ask that the blood of Jesus wipe away every mark of reproach whether physical or spiritual.

10. Under the covering of the Blood of Jesus Christ, I ask for the blood of Jesus to erase every evil and negative name I was ever called.

DAY 19

The Breaking Point

Then shall thy light break forth as the morning, and thine health shall spring forth speedily: and thy righteousness shall go before thee; the glory of the LORD shall be thy reward. Then shalt thou call, and the LORD shall answer; thou shalt cry, and he shall say, Here I am. If thou take away from the midst of thee the yoke, the putting forth of the finger, and speaking vanity
Isaiah 58:8-9 -

FASTING PREPARES OUR HEARTS for God to visit. It humbles us, breaks us, and draws our spirit beings closer to the Maker. When we fast, we add force to our prayers and place a civil demand on our God, as Jacob did when he cried out through the night hours to the dawning of the morning:

They kept on wrestling until the man said, 'Let go of me! It's almost daylight.' And Jacob replied, 'You can't go until you bless me' - Genesis 32:26

Your Light Will Break-Forth

From our devotional reading today, we understand that when we fast God's way, He will speedily interpose.

- You shall call and God will answer. Our prayers will carry urgency and Heaven will be at our disposal.
- The full strength and the unlimited resources of our LORD shall be available to us speedily when we call.
- Fasting truly causes our spirit beings to unite with the infinite riches of our LORD, so that whatever is His is made immediately available to us.
- Our LORD is waiting for us during this season to cry, so that HE can say, "Here I AM".

PRAYER GUIDE 19:

- Pray that as you fast through the month of February, your voice will be remembered in the divine throne room daily.
- Pray that you shall be famous in the presence of the LORD throughout this season.
- Pray that the Spirit of God will carry your prayers with urgency and angelic activities will be operational.

- Pray that the Heavens will be opened this year upon you and the full resources of our Father will be poured upon you in Jesus' name.
- Pray that your spirit will be united and be in uniformity with the Holy Spirit, and you shall be nearer to Him than ever.
- Pray that the I AM God, our Father will fulfill His covenant over your life.

LOG-OFF: DAY 19 – Evening Prayers

Make this confession boldly:

You are my Lord and my God. I know from Your Word that a broken spirit, a broken and a contrite heart are sacrifices, O God, that You will not despise.
I come before you now to offer myself to you Lord God – all of me – my body, my mind and my soul. All I have, all I am, are Yours and Yours alone.
O Lord God, as I submit myself to you, I commit to doing everything I do, to saying everything I say, and to choosing everything I choose, for the sake of Your Kingdom and not mine.

Stand on these prayer points for five minutes each as necessary to pray:

1. Under the covering of the Blood of Jesus Christ, I am committed to my pastors, especially their welfare and the progress of the ministry.
2. Under the covering of the Blood of Jesus Christ, I am committed to the fellowship of the brethren.
3. Under the covering of the Blood of Jesus Christ, I destroy the forces responsible for every lack of commitment in my life up until now. Henceforth anything I start, I am committed to finish it.
4. Under the covering of the Blood of Jesus Christ, anything I say I am committed to doing it.
5. Under the covering of the Blood of Jesus Christ, anything I do I am committed to doing my best. I receive fresh grace for commitment.
6. Under the covering of the Blood of Jesus Christ, I confess that our church workers are committed to their duties.

7. Under the covering of the Blood of Jesus Christ, I will not abandon the duties committed into my hands by God and my Overseer.
8. Under the covering of the Blood of Jesus Christ, I am committed to ensuring that the vision of the local assembly is achieved at all costs.
9. Under the covering of the Blood of Jesus Christ, I believe and confess that the grace of God is sufficient for me.
10. Under the covering of the Blood of Jesus Christ, I boldly declare that everything I am and have is for the kingdom of God.

DAY 20
The Light Shines In Darkness

If you pour yourself out for the hungry and satisfy the desire of the afflicted, then shall your light rise in the darkness and your gloom be as the noonday. And the LORD will guide you continually and satisfy your desire in scorched places and make your bones strong; and you shall be like a watered garden, like a spring of water, whose waters do not fail. – Isaiah 58:10-11

DAY 20 – The Light Shines In Darkness

Pray for the opportunity to share your faith this week with someone who does not have a relationship with Jesus. Pray that God would open the doors and align your path with someone who needs the power and salvation of a new relationship with the Lord. Pray that God would give you the courage to share when the door opens.

LOG-ON: Day 20 – Morning Prayer

1. Under the covering of the Blood of Jesus Christ, Father, use me as your battle axe in my family, my community and in this country to draw lost souls unto your Kingdom, in Jesus' name.
2. Under the covering of the Blood of Jesus Christ, Father, contend with every power contending with the souls of men in my family, in New York and in the USA, and that is preventing them from knowing you, in the mighty name of Jesus Christ.
3. Under the covering of the Blood of Jesus Christ, Father, destroy every work of the devil manifesting against the Gospel in this land in Jesus' name.
4. Lord, use me to win souls all around me in Jesus' name.
5. Under the covering of the Blood of Jesus Christ, Father, make me a worthy laborer in your Kingdom for the harvest of lost souls back unto you in Jesus' name.
6. Under the covering of the Blood of Jesus Christ, Father, let every evil veil covering the eyes of my unsaved family members from confessing Jesus Christ be torn in Jesus' name.

7. Under the covering of the Blood of Jesus Christ, Father, let every hold and deceit of the devil upon the lives of the people in this land preventing them from receiving the gospel be destroyed today in Jesus' name.
8. Under the covering of the Blood of Jesus Christ, Lord, let the activities of the devil cease in this community in Jesus' name.
9. Under the covering of the Blood of Jesus Christ, I decree and declare the life gate of salvation to be opened in our immediate church community in Jesus' name.
10. Under the covering of the Blood of Jesus Christ, any satanic power resisting the penetrating of the gospel in this community, the fire of the Holy Ghost is against you today in Jesus' name.

DAY 20

The Light Shines In Darkness

if you pour yourself out for the hungry and satisfy the desire of the afflicted, then shall your light rise in the darkness and your gloom be as the noonday. And the LORD will guide you continually and satisfy your desire in scorched places and make your bones strong; and you shall be like a watered garden, like a spring of water, whose waters do not fail. – Isaiah 58:10-11

WHEN WE FAST GOD'S WAY, we receive oil for our light. The Spirit of God gains grounds in our lives, and we begin to look more like Him. The more time we spend with Him, affects our being and translates us into His translucent likeness.

Fasting Will Ignite Your Light To Shine In Darkness:

> *The people who walked in darkness have seen a great light; those who dwelt in the land of the shadow of death, upon them a light has shined. Isaiah 9:2*

> *I will also give You as a light to the Gentiles, that You should be My salvation to the ends of the earth. – Isaiah 49:6*
>
> *ARISE, shine; for your light has come! And the glory of the LORD is risen upon you. – Isaiah 60:1*

God's Prolonged Blessing will emerge through fasting and consecration (vv. 10b-11).

- Your light will shine in obscurity: You shall be known and called upon in unknown places.
- Your darkness will be turned into noonday: After this fasting, God will deliver many from situations that we never thought we could rise from. Things will be brighter and we shall burst out in hope.
- That dark problem will turn into your brightest opportunity and success.
- The LORD will continually guide you: No longer will trouble meet you in an uncertain future. This fasting will secure your divine protection for the rest of the year.
- The LORD will satisfy you soul in drought: Financial increase and abundance of resources shall be your portion after this fasting. The LORD will meet all your needs and you shall never know lack after this fast.
- Your bones will be fat: You shall prosper and your territory shall be enlarged this year. The LORD will nourish you and place you on a prosperous pedestal.
- You shall be like a watered garden: Rest assured, this is a glorious year and as you complete this season of fasting with the LORD, you shall be planted by many waters where you will never lack opportunities and divine supply.

PRAYER GUIDE 20:

- Pray that the LORD will cause your light to shine in obscurity and you shall be known and called upon in unknown places.
- Pray that any darkness in your life; in any aspect of your social and spiritual life be turned into noonday immediately.
- Pray that any trouble or crisis you find yourself involved in shall be terminated by angelic operations now.
- Pray for divine guidance and exemption from any impending danger in Jesus' name.
- Pray that you shall be covered and protected for the duration of this year and no evil or harm shall meet you.
- Pray that the LORD God will satisfy you in any spiritual drought or physical drought in which you find yourself.
- Pray that there shall be a divine visitation in every area of your life where you're facing lack and financial liquidation.
- Pray that the LORD shall supply every need in your life this year in Jesus' name.
- Pray that the LORD will open doors of prosperity for you this year and you shall occupy your God given territory and enjoy your possessions in Jesus' name.
- Pray that this is the year in which you shall be fruitful, in which you shall be planted upon many waters and in which you shall enjoy the best of this land in Jesus' name.

LOG-OFF: Day 20 – Evening Prayer

Spend time to make these confessions and declarations over your life. You may pray each prayer point for five minutes if needed:

1. Under the covering of the Blood of Jesus Christ, Father, grant me the desires of my heart according to your will this year, in Jesus' name.
2. Under the covering of the Blood of Jesus Christ, Father, according to your will and your riches in Glory, supply all my needs, in Jesus' name.
3. Under the covering of the Blood of Jesus Christ, Father, whatever I lack now, make a way for me and grant me divine provisions now in Jesus' name.
4. Under the covering of the Blood of Jesus Christ, Father, let the thing (job, business, gift) that gives me my daily bread never be cut away in Jesus' name.
5. Under the covering of the Blood of Jesus Christ, Father, release your blessing in my life this year that would make men glorify your name, in Jesus' name.
6. Under the covering of the Blood of Jesus Christ, Lord, open up your heavens and bless me with the blessing that will make me rich in every area of my life without sorrow, in Jesus' name.
7. Under the covering of the Blood of Jesus Christ, Father, let the source of my financial income never go dry, in Jesus' name.
8. Under the covering of the Blood of Jesus Christ, Father, bless my basket and bless my waters.
9. Under the covering of the Blood of Jesus Christ, Father, as I go out looking for my daily bread, I

will not become a prey to the enemy in Jesus' name.
10. Under the covering of the Blood of Jesus Christ, I boldly confess that my great commission has come, my change has come, my transformation is here, my lifting has come. New things are happening in my life. This is my time and my season. I shall never remain the same again in Jesus' name. Amen.

DAY 21
Kingdom Transformers

And your ancient ruins shall be rebuilt; you shall raise up the foundations of many generations; you shall be called the repairer of the breach, the restorer of streets to dwell in
Isaiah 58:12

DAY 21 – Kingdom Transformers

Pray for Divine Visitation and Encounter. Pray that the presence of God will complete you this year and bring fulfillment in all you do. You will end this year satisfied and in peace for the glory of God. God will comfort you on all sides this year and cause you to walk from one glory into another.

LOG-ON: DAY 21 – Morning Prayers

Begin praying these prayer points through the morning and afternoon. You can spend five minutes on each as necessary:

1. In the year of Joseph's visitation, they hurriedly brought him out of prison, hurriedly changed his prison garments, hurriedly ushered him to the presence of king pharaoh, VIPs, dignitaries, and the presidential environment. They hurriedly gave him a position that he had dreamt about all his life - nations bowing for him. Under the covering of the Blood of Jesus Christ, let my dreams, yearnings, and aspirations be hurriedly fulfilled this year. I come against delay in my life this year.
2. In the year of David's visitation, they hurriedly brought him from the farm and anointed him as a king. Under the covering of the Blood of Jesus Christ, let me be anointed for my purpose. Let me experience divine elevation - from a farmer to a king would be good. From a relief staff to Director, or the owner of a thriving business is my prayer.
3. In the year of Abraham's visitation, he entertained angels and blessings came after they had eaten pepper soup in his vineyard and the word of comfort came to his life. Under the covering of the Blood of Jesus Christ, let me be hospitable. Let me bless the people of God. Let

heaven remember my overdue promise.
4. Under the covering of the Blood of Jesus Christ, In the year of Sarah's visitation, the Lord visited Sarah and she conceived Gen. 21:1-2. This year my Lord will visit me and I will conceive and I will bear a son. This year, I will conceive the ministry, the calling, the talent, the treasure I am believing God for. The idea for that business shall come to me. The anointing for that ministry shall be deposited in me. The idea for that invention shall come to me. The book in my head will be written for this generation and beyond.
5. Under the covering of the Blood of Jesus Christ, Father, grant me the desires of my heart according to your will this year in Jesus' name.
6. Under the covering of the Blood of Jesus Christ, Father, according to your will, supply all my needs for to your Glory in Jesus' name.
7. Under the covering of the Blood of Jesus Christ, Father, for whatever I lack now; make a way for me and grant me divine provisions now in Jesus' name.
8. Under the covering of the Blood of Jesus Christ, Father, let the thing (job, business, gift) that gives me my daily bread never be cut away in Jesus' Name.
9. Under the covering of the Blood of Jesus Christ, Father, release your blessing that would make men to glorify your name in my life this year in Jesus' name.
10. Under the covering of the Blood of Jesus Christ, Lord, open up your heavens and bless me with the blessing that would make me rich in every area of my life without sorrow in Jesus' name.

DAY 21
Kingdom Transformers

And your ancient ruins shall be rebuilt; you shall raise up the foundations of many generations; you shall be called the repairer of the breach, the restorer of streets to dwell in
Isaiah 58:12

COMMUNITY TRANSFORMERS, City Shakers, and Nation Gate Keepers will rise out of this consecrated Fast - Your Posterity Is Blessed (vv. 12).

- **They that be of thee shall build:** Your children, both spiritual and natural offspring shall be builders of houses and properties. They shall never be borrowers and wanderers in a foreign land.
- **Your children shall be restorers:** Where you failed, they will succeed; where you were disgraced, they

shall be graced; and where you stopped, they shall complete.
- **Your children shall raise up foundations:** What you couldn't lift, your children, both spiritual and natural ones, will come and lift-up. Your foundation will never be left desecrated and desolate, but your children will come and build upon it. Your legacy and impact will never be forgotten as the LORD will bless your children forevermore.
- **The Rise of Destiny Builders** – God is calling you to be a builder of whatever is destroyed in your life, your family, community, city and nation. That which was destroyed and left in ruins shall be restored and built up because the LORD will make you a vessel of restoration to the world.
- **Foundation Diggers** – This generation and the next generation are waiting for you to raise a standard and to set the tone for godliness and Kingdom living.
- **The Repairer of the Breach** – For us to experience transformation and revival, someone must rise to repair the breach, to remove the hindrances to God's mandate upon the earth, and to mend the breach between God and humanity. There will be denominational unity and strong affinity among Christians around the world.
- **Restorer of Streets** – God is calling for market-place evangelists to affect the workplaces, the byways, highways, and all street corners with the gospel. They will be called out of the streets and sent back into the streets to impact it with divine power. Through them, hope is coming to the streets and salvation is visiting the streets.

PRAYER GUIDE 21:

- Pray that your children shall be builders in many nations and they shall be possessors of lands and houses in Jesus' name.
- Pray that the LORD shall prosper your lineage and your children will never borrow and be wanderers in Jesus' name.
- Pray that your children and lineage shall be restorers of desolate places and restores of lives in Jesus' name.
- Pray that your children shall raise up many foundations and God will cause your name to be famous.
- Pray for the security of your children's future and make a covenant with God for their posterity.
- Pray that you shall be the repairer of the breach – to amend the relationship between your friends, loved ones, family, and strangers with God.
- Pray that you shall lift up the foundations of many generations – that God will use you to affect this generation and the next for His Glory.
- Pray that you shall be termed a restorer of paths and houses to live in – that through you the lives of many shall be restored, and destinies will experience divine transformation.

LOG-OFF: Day 21 – Evening Prayers

Confession:
The LORD is my light and my salvation; whom shall I fear? the LORD is the strength of my life; of whom shall I be afraid? When the wicked, even mine enemies and my foes, came upon me to eat up my flesh, they stumbled and fell. Though an host should encamp against me, my heart shall not fear: though war should rise against me, in this will I be confident. (Psalm 27:1-3).

Take these confessions and declarations into prayers (Spend five minutes each as necessary):

1. Under the covering of the Blood of Jesus Christ, all arrangements of the devil concerning my destiny, my church, my family, my friends and loved ones, shall not stand; neither shall they come to pass, in the name of Jesus.
2. Under the covering of the Blood of Jesus Christ, I destroy all efforts of the enemy to frustrate my destiny, my family, my church, my friends, and nation in the name of Jesus.
3. Under the covering of the Blood of Jesus Christ, I nullify every writing, agreement or covenant against my life, my family, my church, my friends and my nation, in the name of Jesus.
4. Under the covering of the Blood of Jesus Christ, Father Lord, increase my greatness and comfort me on every side, in the name of Jesus.
5. Under the covering of the Blood of Jesus Christ, O Lord, as You delight in my prosperity, I pray that You bless me indeed in my life. Let no household enemy be able to control my well-being any longer, in the name of Jesus.

6. Under the covering of the Blood of Jesus Christ, let all those who are against me, my family, my church, and my nation without a cause be turned back and be brought to confusion, in the name of Jesus.
7. Under the covering of the Blood of Jesus Christ, I close every door through which the enemies have been working against my life, my family, my church and my nation, in the name of Jesus.
8. Under the covering of the Blood of Jesus Christ, my life is hidden with Christ in God, therefore nobody can kill me or harm me, in the name of Jesus.
9. Under the covering of the Blood of Jesus Christ, I open wide all doors leading to my blessings, victory and breakthroughs which the enemies have closed, in the name of Jesus.
10. Under the covering of the Blood of Jesus Christ, let every territorial spirit working against us in our neighborhood be frustrated, bound and cast out, in the name of Jesus.

DAY 22
The Repairer of the Breach

"And your ancient ruins shall be rebuilt; you shall raise up the foundations of many generations; **you shall be called the repairer of the breach,** the restorer of streets to dwell in." – Isaiah 58:12

DAY 22: The Repairer of the Breach

This marks the twenty-second day of our Consecration Fasting and Prayer. In this devotion, we will respond to the heavenly call for Repairers of the Breach. Who are they? And why does this generation need the Repairers? We begin this devotion with our morning prayers:

LOG-ON: DAY 22 – Morning Prayers

Make this confession for five minutes each as necessary:

1. Under the covering of the Blood of Jesus Christ, I immerse myself in the Blood of Jesus Christ: I saturate my spirit, conscience, intuition and worship.
2. Under the covering of the Blood of Jesus Christ, I saturate my soul: conscious, sub-conscious, and unconscious. I also saturate my mind, will, emotions, and intellect.
3. Under the covering of the Blood of Jesus Christ, I saturate my five senses: sight, hearing, smell, taste, and touch.
4. Under the covering of the Blood of Jesus Christ, I saturate my physical body: brain, physical appetites, and sexual character.
5. Under the covering of the Blood of Jesus Christ, I cover my doorpost and possessions with the Blood of Jesus Christ (Exod. 12:13).
6. Under the covering of the Blood of Jesus Christ, I overcome the devil through the Blood of Jesus Christ (Rev. 12:11).
7. Under the covering of the Blood of Jesus Christ, I sprinkle the Blood of Jesus Christ and receive multiplied grace and peace (1 Pet. 1:2).

8. Under the covering of the Blood of Jesus Christ, I am made perfect through the Blood of the Everlasting Covenant (Heb 13:20-21).
9. Under the covering of the Blood of Jesus Christ, I have boldness to enter into the presence of God through the Blood of Jesus Christ (Heb. 10:19).
10. Under the covering of the Blood of Jesus Christ, my conscience is purged from dead works to serve the living God through the Blood of Jesus Christ (Heb. 9:14).

DAY 22
Repairer of the Breach Part 1

"And your ancient ruins shall be rebuilt; you shall raise up the foundations of many generations; you shall be called the repairer of the breach, the restorer of streets to dwell in." – Isaiah 58:12

IN THIS SEASON OF CONSECRATION, God will raise you to be a Repairer of the Breach, the Restorer of Paths to dwell in.

- **Breach** (Dictionary): An opening made by breaking down something solid; gap; alienation; estrangement; to take the place of someone missing, or unable to act in an emergency. A breaking of a promise
- **Breach** (Bible) A bursting forth or breach; transgression, breach of trust or to break open

- **Repair** (Dictionary): To put into good condition again; to mend; to make up for or remedy
- **Repair** (Bible): To renew, restore or healing and restoration

Whenever I think of a breach, it is either a breach of a contract or the breaching of a city wall by an army. God's Word covers several meanings for breach:

1. God took a strong stand on a breach of trust. In the Exodus account, the breach would be taking what does not belong to you.

   For every breach of trust, whether it is for ox, for donkey, for sheep, for clothing, or for any lost thing about which one says, 'This is it,' the case of both parties shall come before the judges; he whom the judges condemn shall pay double to his neighbor. – Exodus 22:9 (NASB)

Prayer Topic:
- Have you broken trust in any area of your life with God? It's time to pray and repair that breach with God.
- Have you broken trust with a friend who trusted you with a situation, and this has damaged your relationship? Pray for restoration and a sealing of that breach.

LOG-OFF: DAY 22 – Evening Prayers

Pray to close up every breach and hedge (Spend at least five minutes each on each point):

1. Under the covering of the Blood of Jesus Christ, my heart is sprinkled with the Blood of Jesus Christ from an evil conscience (Heb. 10:22).
2. Under the covering of the Blood of Jesus Christ, every strategy of hell is exposed and brought to light.
3. Under the covering of the Blood of Jesus Christ, I receive the plans of God for my life; thoughts of peace and not evil that bring me an expected end (Jer.29:11).
4. Under the covering of the Blood of Jesus Christ, I am delivered from every satanic trap and plot against my life, family, ministry, church, city and nation in the name of Jesus.
5. Under the covering of the Blood of Jesus Christ, I release the whirlwind to scatter those that would conspire against me, my family, ministry, church, city and nation in the name of Jesus.
6. Under the covering of the Blood of Jesus Christ, they are turned back and brought to confusion that devise my hurt in the name of Jesus.
7. Under the covering of the Blood of Jesus Christ, the nets they have hidden catch them and into that very destruction they fall.
8. Under the covering of the Blood of Jesus Christ, I bind and rebuke every spirit of Sanballat and Tobiah in the name of Jesus (Neh. 6:1-6).
9. Under the covering of the Blood of Jesus Christ, I am hidden from the secret counsel of the wicked, in the name of Jesus.
10. Under the covering of the Blood of Jesus Christ, I break and divide every demonic confederacy against my life, family, ministry and Church, in the name of Jesus.

DAY 23

Repairer of the Breach Part 2

"And your ancient ruins shall be rebuilt; you shall raise up the foundations of many generations; **you shall be called the repairer of the breach,** the restorer of streets to dwell in." Isaiah 58:12

DAY 23: Repairer of the Breach Part 2

This marks the twenty-second day of our Consecration Fasting and Prayer. In this devotion we will continue our inquisition of the Repairers of the Breach. Who are they? And why does this generation need the Repairers? We begin this devotion with our morning prayers:

LOG-ON: DAY 23 – Morning Prayers

Pray to close up every breach and hedge (Spend at least five minutes each on each point):

1. Under the covering of the Superior Blood of Jesus Christ, I close up any breach in my life that would give Satan and demons access, in the name of Jesus Christ (Eccl.10:8).
2. Under the covering of the Superior Blood of Jesus Christ, I decree that every hedge broken in my life is restored, in the name of Jesus Christ (Eccl.10:8).
3. Under the covering of the Superior Blood of Jesus Christ, I stand in the gap and make up the hedge for my family, my church, and my nation (Ezek.22:30).
4. Under the covering of the Superior Blood of Jesus Christ, I repent and receive forgiveness for any sin that has opened the door for any spirit to enter and operate in my life, family, ministry or Church, in the name of Jesus Christ (Eph.4:27).
5. Under the covering of the Superior Blood of Jesus Christ, I am a rebuilder of the wall, and a repairer of the breach (Isa.58:12).
6. Under the covering of the Superior Blood of Jesus Christ, I RENOUNCE ALL TWISTED SPEECH THAT WOULD CAUSE A BREACH, IN THE NAME OF JESUS CHRIST (Prov. 15:4).
7. Under the covering of the Superior Blood of Jesus Christ, I destroy all spoken curses and negative words that I have spoken over my life in the name of Jesus Christ.

8. Under the covering of the Superior Blood of Jesus Christ, I destroy all spoken curses and negative words spoken over my life by others, including those in authority, in the name of Jesus Christ.
9. Under the covering of the Superior Blood of Jesus Christ, I destroy and disannul all ungodly covenants, oaths, and pledges I have made with my lips, in the name of Jesus Christ.
10. Under the covering of the Superior Blood of Jesus Christ, I bind up all my breaches, O LORD (Isa. 30:26).

DAY 23
Repairer of the Breach Part 2

"And your ancient ruins shall be rebuilt; you shall raise up the foundations of many generations; you shall be called the repairer of the breach, the restorer of streets to dwell in." Isaiah 58:12

ISAIAH CHAPTER 58 EXPLAINS who the repairers of the breach are. According to the scriptures they are watchmen who cry aloud and spare not.

The word breach in the phrase "the repairer of the breach" means according to the Hebrew **"a break," or "a gap"**.

Another important view of breaching is noted here in the scriptures:

> *They made a calf in Horeb, And worshiped the molded image. Thus they changed their glory Into the image of an ox that eats grass. They forgot God their Savior, Who had done great things in Egypt, Wondrous works in the land of Ham, Awesome things by the Red Sea. Therefore He said that He would destroy them, Had not Moses His chosen one stood before Him in the breach, To turn away His wrath, lest He destroy them.*
> – Psalm 106:19-23 (NKJV)

This breach was a place where Moses stood between God and Israel to intercede. Had Moses not stepped in, God's wrath would have gone forth and destroyed the entire nation! In fact, God told Moses that He would use Moses to create another nation. Nevertheless, Moses stood in the breaches on behalf of the people, so that God will spare them. May God grant us the boldness to stand in the breaches for our families, cities and nations during this consecration period. If you see the judgment of God upon any person or peoples, will you stand in the gap for them?

Prayer Topic:

- Look around you – Do you know anyone who needs you to stand in the gap or breaches for them? Mention their name or names now and pray for them. It could be your own child, your mother, your father, or a friend?

- Look at the policies, and the ways of your city and nation and if there's a transgress (a breach of God's ways and law), then start now and stand in the gap for where you dwell, that mercy will triumph over divine judgment. Like Moses and Abraham, make your voice count during this period, that God will spare us judgment and send power of conviction and deliverance on a national-scale.

LOG-OFF: DAY 23 – Evening Prayers

Spend some time praying these prayers. If possible, spend at least five minutes on each prayer point:

1. Under the covering of the Superior Blood of Jesus Christ, I put on the full armor of God, NOW, in the name of Jesus Christ (Eph 6:11).
2. Under the covering of the Superior Blood of Jesus Christ, I ask for and thank You, Father God, for placing the cloak of humility over me, in the name of Jesus Christ.
3. Under the covering of the Superior Blood of Jesus Christ, I decree a hedge of protection around my mind, body, family, finances, possessions and ministry, in the name of Jesus Christ. LORD, turn every curse spoken against my life into a blessing, in the name of Jesus Christ (Neh.13:2).
4. Under the covering of the Superior Blood of Jesus Christ, Oh LORD, let the breach in my church and my family be sealed up now, in Jesus' name.
5. Under the covering of the Superior Blood of Jesus Christ, every wall erected by the enemy against my life, family, ministry and Church is DESTROYED NOW, in the name of Jesus (Ezek.13:14).
6. Under the covering of the Superior Blood of Jesus Christ, I destroy every altar erected by the enemy against my life, family, ministry and Church in the name of Jesus (Hos.10:2).
7. Under the covering of the Superior Blood of Jesus Christ, I break and destroy every demonic blockage and barrier of the enemy to hinder the will and plans of God for my life, family, ministry and Church, in the name of Jesus.
8. Under the covering of the Superior Blood of Jesus Christ, Your kingdom come, Your will be done, in

my life, family, ministry, church, and city according to Your plan, O Lord.
9. Under the covering of the Superior Blood of Jesus Christ, Your kingdom advances in my city and is established through preaching, teaching, and healing (Matt.4:23).
10. Under the covering of the Superior Blood of Jesus Christ, The gates of my life and city are NOW opened for the KING OF GLORY TO COME IN (Psa. 24:7).

DAY 24

Repairer of the Breach Part 3

"And your ancient ruins shall be rebuilt; you shall raise up the foundations of many generations; **you shall be called the repairer of the breach,** the restorer of streets to dwell in." – Isaiah 58:12

DAY 24: The Repairers of the Breach

We are almost done with the fast. Today is the twenty-fourth day of the Consecration Fasting and Prayer. In this devotion we will continue our prayers on the Repairers of the Breach. Who are they? And why does this generation need the Repairers? We begin this devotion with our morning prayers:

LOG-ON: Day 24 – Morning Prayers

Father, we come to You in the name of our Lord and Savior Jesus Christ (spend five minutes on each prayer-point as necessary):

1. Under the covering of the Superior Blood of Jesus Christ, because of our sins and disobedience, our land and people have been cursed. But You are a merciful God, full of grace and love, and we ask that You forgive us our sins and cleanse us of all unrighteousness.
2. Under the covering of the Superior Blood of Jesus Christ, O Lord, hear our prayers, open Your eyes, and see our despair.
3. Under the covering of the Superior Blood of Jesus Christ, O Lord, hear! O Lord, forgive! O Lord, listen and act! Do not delay for Your own sake, my God, for Your people are called by Your name. Break the curses that have come upon our land and people, we humbly ask, O God.
4. Under the covering of the Superior Blood of Jesus Christ, we bind all ruler spirits Satan has sent to carry out those curses against us, in Jesus Christ's name. Your Word says whatever we bind on earth will be bound in heaven, and whatever we loose on earth will be loosed in heaven (See Matthew 16:19; 18:18).
5. Under the covering of the Superior Blood of Jesus Christ, OH LORD, free the souls of men, women and children who have been bound by Satan, and take the blinders off their minds.

6. Under the covering of the Superior Blood of Jesus Christ, OH LORD, we humbly ask You to send angels from heaven to overrule all of Satan's ruler spirits that control our land and people.
7. Under the covering of the Superior Blood of Jesus Christ, we cut all the cords of the enemy and cast them away and dry up the river of jealousy, in our families and churches in Jesus Christ's name.
8. Under the covering of the Superior Blood of Jesus Christ, hide us beneath Your wings and cover us with Your feathers to protect us against the enemy. "He will cover you with His feathers, and under His wings you will find refuge" (Psalm 91:4).
9. Under the covering of the Superior Blood of Jesus Christ, in the Name of JESUS CHRIST, I cover myself, family and Church with the Blood of Jesus Christ. I ask for the LORD of Host to protect us.
10. Under the covering of the Superior Blood of Jesus Christ, as Your War Club and Weapons of War: I break down, undam, destroy, and blow up all walls of protection around all witches, warlocks, wizards, satanists, sorcerers, psychics and the like, operating against my family and church in Jesus' name.

DAY 24
Repairer of the Breach Part 3

"And your ancient ruins shall be rebuilt; you shall raise up the foundations of many generations; you shall be called the repairer of the breach, the restorer of streets to dwell in." – Isaiah 58:12

THE REPAIRERS OF THE BREACH are laborers in the hands of God, to lose the bonds of wickedness, undo the heavy burdens, and break every yoke that binds mankind in sin.

"***Breach***" has a very interesting usage in the English language as it pertains to our relationship with God and the church's present state.

- Here is a list of synonyms for "breach" taken from *The Reader's Digest Oxford Complete Word Finder*: "break, gap, opening, rupture, split, alienation, schism."

The first definition for *breach* is unusually appropriate as far as the situation in the church is concerned: "the breaking of, or failure to observe a law or contract or standard."

We have a covenant; a contract, with God, and He has given us a standard. This sounds a great deal like I John 3:4: "Sin [which separates, creates a breach] is the transgression of the law."

- The second definition of *breach* is also rich: "A breaking of relations; an estrangement; a quarrel, a broken state."

Together, these describe almost exactly what has happened to the church as a result of breaking the covenant (as a result of breaking laws, as a result of sin). There has been a breaking of relations with God because of the church's failure, as a body, to live up to the contract that we made with Him.

- Spiritually **"a repairer of breaches"** is one who restores the right way, beginning with him or herself. As a repairer of the breaches, you may have no influence or control over what others do, but you have control over what ***you do***. As a result, when you repair your personal breach with God, the breach in the wall closes a bit. It is as if a stone or a brick were added to the wall—another person is again in a good relationship with God. It's time to repair your own breaches with God.

Read Ezekiel 22:25-30:

> *And I sought for a man among them, that should make up the hedge, and stand in the gap before me for the land, that I should not destroy it: but I found none. (vv.30)*

God is calling us to stand in the gap and build up the walls of our families, cities, churches and nations. May you arise during this season to respond to the heavenly call.

Prayer Topic:

- Do *we* have a wall to keep the enemies of God's way out of our lives and homes? Have we set boundaries against the world, or have we torn down the wall? If we have a wall, are we leaving the gates open and unguarded? Are we willing to *fight* to defend our families and our church? Or do we just let the enemy stream in unchallenged? Are we willing to stand up to the world? Step now into the gap, and pray until all breaches are sealed and the walls are lifted up once again.

- OH GOD, *make us repairers of the breaches, and restorers of streets to dwell in.*

LOG-OFF: DAY 24 – Evening Prayers

Spend some time praying with these prayer points. You can stay on each point for five minutes as needed:

1. Under the covering of the Superior Blood of Jesus Christ, I am sitting in heavenly places in Christ far above all principality, power, might and dominion and every name that is named (Eph. 1:3).
2. Under the covering of the Superior Blood of Jesus Christ, I take my position and authority in the heavens and bind the principalities and powers that operate against my life, family, ministry, church and city, in the name of Jesus.
3. Under the covering of the Superior Blood of Jesus Christ, I destroy every program in the heavens that would operate against me through the sun, moon, stars and constellations in the name of Jesus.
4. Under the covering of the Superior Blood of Jesus Christ, I bind and destroy any ungodly forces operating against my life, family, ministry, church and city through Arcturus, Pleiades, Mazzaroth and Orion. I cut their bands and ask for angelic assistance to remove any bands from my spirit, soul and body now in the name of Jesus (Job 38:31-32).
5. Under the covering of the Superior Blood of Jesus Christ, I bind and disannul all sun and moon deities and demons; operating through the sun and moon in the name of Jesus (2 Kings 23:5).
6. Under the covering of the Superior Blood of Jesus Christ, I bind and disannul all deities and demons operating through the stars and planets in the name of Jesus (2 Kings 23:5).
7. Under the covering of the Superior Blood of Jesus Christ, I bind and disannul the prince of the power of the air over my life and city in the name of Jesus (Eph. 2:2).

8. Under the covering of the Superior Blood of Jesus Christ, I renounce any power of astrology, I renounce palm readings, psychic phenomenal and associations with such evil practitioners. The evil powers of heaven are shaken and bound in the name of Jesus (Matt. 24:29).
9. Under the covering of the Superior Blood of Jesus Christ, the sun shall not smite me by day or the moon by night in the name of Jesus (Psa. 121:6).
10. Under the covering of the Superior Blood of Jesus Christ, I pray for angels to be released to war against any spirit in the heavens assigned to block my prayers from being answered in the name of Jesus (Dan. 10:12-13).

DAY 25
The Holy Day

If you turn away your foot from the sabbath, from doing your pleasure on my holy day; and call the sabbath a delight, the holy of the LORD, honorable; and shall honor him, not doing your own ways, nor finding your own pleasure, nor speaking your own words:" - Isaiah 58:13

DAY 25 – The Holy Day

When you desire that new things should begin in your life, the end of your sinful, hopeless, helpless, weary and frustrating life is a new beginning of a vibrant and exciting life in Christ. Isaiah 43:19: *"Behold, I will do a new thing; now it shall spring forth; shall ye not know it?"*

LOG-ON: DAY 25 – Morning Prayers

Spend at least five minutes, confess, declare and pray on each prayer point as necessary:

1. Under the covering of the Blood of Jesus Christ, Oh Father, I ask to know Your mind about . . . (slot in the appropriate situation) situation.

2. Under the covering of the Blood of Jesus Christ, Oh LORD, let the spirit of prophesy and revelation fall upon the totality of my being in the name of Jesus.

3. Under the covering of the Blood of Jesus Christ, Holy Spirit, reveal the deep and secret things to me about . . . .

4. Under the covering of the Blood of Jesus Christ, I bind every demon that pollutes spiritual vision and dreams in the name of Jesus.

5. Under the covering of the Blood of Jesus Christ, let every filth blocking my communication pipe with the living God be washed clean with the blood of Jesus.

6. Under the covering of the Blood of Jesus Christ, I receive power to operate with sharp spiritual eyes that cannot be deceived in the name of Jesus.

7. Under the covering of the Blood of Jesus Christ, let the glory and the power of the Almighty God fall upon my life in a mighty way in the name of Jesus.

8. Under the covering of the Blood of Jesus Christ, I remove my name from the book of those who grope and stumble in darkness in the name of Jesus.

9. Under the covering of the Blood of Jesus Christ, O Lord, make me a vessel capable of knowing Your secret things.

10. Under the covering of the Blood of Jesus Christ, I confess and declare, divine revelations, spiritual visions, dreams and information will not become a scarce commodity in my life in the name of Jesus.

DAY 25

The Holy Day

If you turn away your foot from the sabbath, from doing your pleasure on my holy day; and call the sabbath a delight, the holy of the LORD, honorable; and shall honor him, not doing your own ways, nor finding your own pleasure, nor speaking your own words:" - Isaiah 58:13

WE MUST PLAN TO GIVE to the LORD what belongs to Him. We should consecrate one day of the week, to be given wholly to the LORD. The Shabbat or the Sabbath, is holy in the Old Covenant. In the New Covenant we deem Sunday to be our Shabbat, and this day must be kept holy, which is to say, set apart for the LORD. It is the first day of the week, and it should be given to the LORD as a tithe for the rest of what we are to expect in the week:

God's Delight: Keep the Shabbat (v. 13)

- During this fasting make a covenant with the LORD that you shall keep and be faithful to the Sabbath, which in this case is Sunday, the appointed day for the gathering of the saints or brethren.
- Be desirous that you will be a faithful tithe payer, and a consistent member in the house of God.
- Pray if your job hinders you from joining the LORD's day. This is an opportunity to use this fasting and pray that God will make provision for a better job so you can be at church always.
- God is still blessing the Jews because they have kept the covenant of the Sabbath. Now how much more and greatly the LORD will bless those who are saved under the New Testament, if we can also be faithful to the LORD's day of service and give unto the LORD what rightly belongs to Him.

PRAYER GUIDE 25:

- Pray that the Spirit of God will develop a love for fellowship in your spirit.
- Pray that you will desire to be in the House of the LORD all the days of your life even as David promised the LORD.
- Pray that you shall never stray from the presence and the House of the LORD but you shall keep the Sabbath (the LORD's day of Service).
- Pray that the LORD will give you a servanthood heart to serve in the House

of the LORD and honor Him for His goodness.
- Pray that the Spirit of the LORD will guide you to win souls into the Kingdom of our Christ.
- Pray that you shall be a soul winner and you shall be known as a disciple of Jesus Christ.
- Pray that God will cause His blessing and eternal glory to fall upon Honeywell Baptist Church on every LORD's day.
- Pray for the pastors and leaders of this church that they will be kept by the LORD and strengthened for the LORD's day.
- Pray for the Praise and worship team and ushering department that God will give them wisdom and abiding knowledge for the service of His house.

LOG-OFF: Day 25 – Evening Prayers

Spend at least five minutes to confess, declare and pray on each prayer point as necessary:

1. Under the covering of the Blood of Jesus Christ, I reject every spiritual contamination, in the name of Jesus.
2. Under the covering of the Blood of Jesus Christ, O Lord, give me power to overcome all obstacles to my breakthroughs.
3. Under the covering of the Blood of Jesus Christ, O Lord, give me divine prescription to my problems.
4. Under the covering of the Blood of Jesus Christ, I break all curses of leaking blessings, in the name of Jesus.
5. Under the covering of the Blood of Jesus Christ, let all spiritual holes in my life be closed with the blood of Jesus, in the name of Jesus.
6. Under the covering of the Blood of Jesus Christ, Lord, help me to locate the defect in the clay of my life.
7. Under the covering of the Blood of Jesus Christ, Lord, let me be in the right place at the right time.
8. Under the covering of the Blood of Jesus Christ, let my enemies pitch their tents against one another, in the name of Jesus.
9. Under the covering of the Blood of Jesus Christ, I frustrate and disappoint every instrument of the enemy fashioned against me, in the name of Jesus.
10. Under the covering of the Blood of Jesus Christ, I seal my victory with the blood of Jesus.

DAY 26
Removing Spiritual Breaches

"And your ancient ruins shall be rebuilt; you shall raise up the foundations of many generations; you shall be called the repairer of the breach, the restorer of streets to dwell in." – Isaiah 58:12

DAY 26 – Removing Spiritual Breaches

When God calls us to fast, we should come before Him, not before man. We should seek God in the fast.

LOG-ON: DAY 26 – Morning Prayers

Spend at least five minutes, confess, declare and pray on each prayer point as necessary:

1. Thank God for the Holy Spirit.
2. Under the covering of the Blood of Jesus Christ, Lord give unto me the Spirit of revelation and wisdom in the knowledge of Yourself.
3. Under the covering of the Blood of Jesus Christ, Holy Spirit remove spiritual cataracts from my eyes.
4. Under the covering of the Blood of Jesus Christ, Lord, forgive me for every false motive or thought that has ever been formed in my heart.
5. Under the covering of the Blood of Jesus Christ, Lord, forgive me for any lie that I have ever told against any person, system or organization.
6. Under the covering of the Blood of Jesus Christ, Lord, deliver me from the bondage and sin of spiritual laziness.
7. Under the covering of the Blood of Jesus Christ, Lord, open up my understanding.
8. Under the covering of the Blood of Jesus Christ, Lord, teach me deep and secret things.
9. Under the covering of the Blood of Jesus, Lord, reveal to me every secret behind any of my problems.
10. Under the covering of the Blood of Jesus Christ, Oh Lord, bring to the light everything planned against me in darkness.

DAY 26

Removing Spiritual Breaches

"And your ancient ruins shall be rebuilt; you shall raise up the foundations of many generations; you shall be called the repairer of the breach, the restorer of streets to dwell in." – Isaiah 58:12

GOD'S PEOPLE are instructed,

> *And they that shall be of thee shall build the old waste places: thou shalt raise up the foundations of many generations; and thou shalt be called, The repairer of the breach, The restorer of paths to dwell in* - (Isa. 58:12).

We have spent time in this fasting learning how we can practically become the repairer of the breach for the church, our families, or for those lost in darkness. What does it mean to build up the old waste places?

As Christians, it is very easy to point fingers at others' weaknesses and faults, and tell other people what they need to change in their lives. It is also easy to tell our fellow leaders how they could be more effective in ministry. But could there possibly be some breaches in our own spiritual wall that might be keeping back the Holy Spirit and hindering our own effectiveness in life?

It's really important that we take time for self-examination, so we know what breaches we have.

As we recognize that the enemy is trying to weaken our spiritual fortress, so he can overcome us and keep us from being fully effective in God's service, we should prayerfully ask the Lord to search our heart (Psalm 139:23, 24). The Bible tells us, *"Examine yourselves, whether ye be in the faith; prove your own selves"* (2 Corinthians 13:5).

Although not exhaustive in its scope, during the days ahead of us, we will deal with a list of common spiritual breaches that hinder the outpouring of the Holy Spirit in our lives.

I encourage you to prayerfully review this list as we come to the final days of our fasting.

Also, as you pray, ask the Lord if there are any other breaches or gaps that are hindering your walk with Him. If we ask with an earnest heart, He will show us! We are told, God's Word is faithful, and He will give you deliverance. (See Hebrews 7:25)

LOG-OFF: DAY 26 – Evening Prayers

Pray to close up every breach and hedge (spend at least five minutes each on each point):

1. Under the covering of the Blood of Jesus Christ, I receive deliverance through the Blood of Jesus Christ (Isa. 54:5).
2. Under the covering of the Blood of Jesus Christ, I receive the fullness of the Holy Spirit and the Anointing through the Blood of Jesus Christ.
3. Under the covering of the Blood of Jesus Christ, the Blood of Jesus Christ bears witness to my deliverance and salvation (1 John 5:8).
4. Under the covering of the Blood of Jesus Christ, the Blood of Jesus Christ cleanses me from all sin (1 John 1:7).
5. Under the covering of the Blood of Jesus Christ, I receive victory through the finished work of Christ Jesus (Heb. 12:4).
6. Under the covering of the Blood of Jesus Christ, I rebuke and cast out all spirits of guilt, shame and condemnation through the Blood of Jesus Christ.
7. Under the covering of the Blood of Jesus Christ, I destroy the power of sin and iniquity in my life through the Blood of Jesus Christ (Heb. 10:17).
8. Under the covering of the Superior Blood of Jesus Christ, I command every breach: BE STOPPED NOW IN THE NAME OF JESUS CHRIST (Neh.4:7).
9. Under the covering of the Superior Blood of Jesus Christ, I command that my walls be salvation and my gates praise (Isa.60:18).
10. Under the covering of the Superior Blood of Jesus Christ, I confess and declare that Christ is my hedge and my salvation.

DAY 27
How To Detect Personal Breaches

"And your ancient ruins shall be rebuilt; you shall raise up the foundations of many generations; you shall be called the repairer of the breach, the restorer of streets to dwell in." – Isaiah 58:12

DAY 27: How to Detect Personal Breaches

We are almost done with the fast. Today is the twenty-seventh day of the Consecration Fasting and Prayer. In this devotion we will continue our prayers on the Repairers of the Breach. Who are they? And why does this generation need the Repairers? We begin this devotion with our morning prayers:

LOG-ON: Day 27 – Morning Prayers

Father, we come to You in the name of our Lord and Savior Jesus Christ (spend five minutes on each prayer-point as necessary):

1. Under the covering of the Superior Blood of Jesus Christ, I surrender to the operations of the Holy Spirit in my life in Jesus' name.
2. Under the covering of the Superior Blood of Jesus Christ, I confess and declare I am free of any seeds of oppression in Jesus' name.
3. Under the covering of the Superior Blood of Jesus Christ, I confess and declare no weapon fashioned against me shall prosper in Jesus' name.
4. Under the covering of the Superior Blood of Jesus Christ, I plead the blood against any voice of the accuser against my life in Jesus' name.
5. Under the covering of the Superior Blood of Jesus Christ, I plead the blood over my mind and receive deliverance from any mental attacks.
6. Under the covering of the Superior Blood of Jesus Christ, O Lord, righteousness belongs to You, but we are ashamed. We, Your people all over the world, have sinned against You.
7. Under the covering of the Superior Blood of Jesus Christ, we confess our sins and the sins of our forefathers. We have sinned against You. We have lived

wickedly, and have rebelled, disobeying Your voice and Your will.
8. Under the covering of the Superior Blood of Jesus Christ, we have allowed ourselves to be deceived and distracted.
9. Under the covering of the Superior Blood of Jesus Christ, we have not walked with the Holy Spirit, whom You gave us to guide us, teach us, and show us all truth. We have become spiritually immature, worldly, and unable to live out the truth. We have failed to do Your will.
10. Under the covering of the Superior Blood of Jesus Christ, we confess and repent of the sins of idolatry, witchcraft, sexual immorality, theft, lying, greed, pride, murder, adultery, dishonoring our parents, unbelief, lack of love, and countless other sins against You, O Lord.

DAY 27

How To Detect Personal Breaches

"And your ancient ruins shall be rebuilt; you shall raise up the foundations of many generations; you shall be called the repairer of the breach, the restorer of streets to dwell in."
– Isaiah 58:12

COMMON BREACHES that hold back the outpouring of the Holy Spirit in our lives:

1. Unconfessed sin: Anything that we have done wrong toward God, toward His law, toward our own body, or toward others and not made right.
- *Promises for those who Confess their sins* (1 John 1:9, 1 Corinthians 15:57)

2. Idols: In this case, I am not talking about "graven

images." I am referring to anything that comes between God and us, or anything that is more important in our lives than our relationship and quality time with God each day. If we have an "idol," it will often consume our attention, focus, and thought-life to the exclusion of other healthy activities, family needs, or ministry tasks. (*Note: Even "ministry" can become an idol if it comes between us and our maintaining a daily relationship connection with God!*)

- *Promises for those who put away Idols* (Ezekiel 36:25-27, Jeremiah 24:7).

3. Addictions: These breaches could be the same as our "idols" or they might be different. An addiction might be a physical substance or food, or a habit or activity that you can't imagine giving up: like being a gossip addict, a TV addict, a social media addict, a pornography addict, an attention or fame addict, or a sugar addict. But if God is to remain the King of our lives, He must be the Lord of our lives! *In fact, He must be our addiction.*

- *Promises for overcoming Addictions* (Luke 18:27, Ps. 55:16-18)

4. Ungodly Mindsets: The most popular ungodly mindsets include, but are not limited to: pride in our achievements and spiritual accomplishments, pride in our talents, pride in our leadership and status, feeling superior over others, arrogance, self-righteousness, selfishness, self-seeking, self-promotion, greed, lusts, jealousy, envy, vanity, gluttony, anxiety, irritability, impatience, anger, bitterness, resentment, unforgiveness, discontentment, unthankfulness, fear, self-pity,

pessimism, doubt toward God, spiritual laziness and apathy, unbelief, hate, victimization, unteachable in spirit, disrespect for those in authority, unholy thoughts and desires, and seeking our own rather than others' best interest.

- *Promises for overcoming Ungodly Mindsets* (Isaiah 26:3, Psalm 119:165, Philippians 4:8).

5. Ungodly Conversations: These breaches are also seldom addressed, yet they are quite prevalent, even in the lives of professing Christians. They include, but are not limited to: gossiping, (even spiritual gossiping while justifying itself with the motive of edifying others can be included), sarcasm, criticism, backbiting, judgementalism, complaining, murmuring, exaggerating tales, lying, inappropriate flirtation, vulgar and foul language, vocalized disrespect, cynicism, expressing doubt toward God, toward the church, toward ministry success, leadership, and more. God tells us, "He that hath no rule over his own spirit is like a city that is broken down, and without walls." (Proverbs 25:28)

- Promises to help overcome Ungodly Conversations (Isaiah 6:5-7, Ephesians 4:22, 23, 29).

It is vital to detect a breach before it is used by the enemy to cause havoc in your life. Truly, there are far too many Christians struggling in life because their spiritual walls are broken. The prophet Jeremiah laments that because the walls of Jerusalem are broken, foxes (enemies) walk upon it (Lamentation 5:18).

Child of God, fix your broken walls. Seal those breaches in your life today. Do the work for your deliverance.

LOG-OFF: Day 27 – Evening Prayers

Spend at least five minutes, confess, declare and pray on each prayer point as necessary:

1. Under the covering of the Blood of Jesus Christ, I declare any emotional breach is sealed in my life in Jesus' name.
2. Under the covering of the Blood of Jesus Christ, I plead the blood against any breaches in my spiritual life that attracts demonic assaults, in Jesus' name.
3. Under the covering of the Blood of Jesus Christ, I withdraw all my benefits from the hands of the oppressors, in the name of Jesus.
4. Under the covering of the Blood of Jesus Christ, let all unprofitable marks in my life be erased, in Jesus' Name.
5. Under the covering of the Blood of Jesus Christ, let every power chasing away my blessings be paralyzed, in the name of Jesus.
6. Under the covering of the Blood of Jesus Christ, let every good thing eaten up by the enemy be vomited now, in the name of Jesus.
7. Under the covering of the Blood of Jesus Christ, let the anointing for spiritual breakthroughs fall upon me, in the name of Jesus.
8. Under the covering of the Blood of Jesus Christ, O Lord, make me a prayer addict.
9. Under the covering of the Blood of Jesus Christ, O Lord, ignite my prayer life with your fire.
10. Under the covering of the Blood of Jesus Christ, O Lord, empower my prayer altar.

DAY 28
How To Detect Personal Breaches II

"And your ancient ruins shall be rebuilt; you shall raise up the foundations of many generations; you shall be called the repairer of the breach, the restorer of streets to dwell in." – Isaiah 58:12

DAY 28–How To Detect Personal Breaches II

We must continue to examine ourselves during the fasting. You should not complete this fast without doing due diligence for yourself. You cannot afford to end it unaccomplished. Do it the right way now.

LOG-ON: DAY 28 – Morning Prayers

Spend at least five minutes, confess, declare and pray on each prayer point as necessary:

1. Under the covering of the Superior Blood of Jesus Christ, I yield myself to the operation of the Holy Spirit in my life.
2. Under the covering of the Superior Blood of Jesus Christ, I confess that I belong to the LORD, I am a child of Christ, I am saved, I am delivered, and my future is great.
3. Under the covering of the Superior Blood of Jesus Christ, I confess and declare the spirit of fear has no place in my life in Jesus' name.
4. Under the covering of the Superior Blood of Jesus Christ, I reject any seeds of gossips sown by anyone about anyone into my life, in Jesus' name.
5. Under the covering of the Superior Blood of Jesus Christ, I rebel and refuse to be a vessel for the devil to use to destroy anyone in Jesus' name.
6. Under the covering of the Blood of Jesus Christ, Oh Lord, ignite and revive my beneficial potentials.
7. Under the covering of the Blood of Jesus Christ, Oh Lord give me divine wisdom to operate my life.

8. Under the covering of the Blood of Jesus Christ, Oh Lord make our Church a citadel of holiness, wonder, miracle and glory upon the earth.
9. Under the covering of the Blood of Jesus Christ, Oh LORD bring to our church your choicest workers and keep all other evil agents away.
10. Under the covering of the Blood of Jesus Christ, O Lord, let every veil preventing me from having plain spiritual vision be removed.

DAY 28

How To Detect Personal Breaches II

"And your ancient ruins shall be rebuilt; you shall raise up the foundations of many generations; you shall be called the repairer of the breach, the restorer of streets to dwell in." – Isaiah 58:12

WITH JUST TWO DAYS TO THE END of the fasting, we conclude here with five additional indications that there is a breach in one's personal life. Carefully, examine yourself, and pray accordingly that the LORD will seal these breaches or gaps in your physical, emotional, and spiritual life.

6. Ungodly Behaviors: Some of these breaches may be quite normal in the society in which we live, but they are not acceptable to God. These behaviors

include, but are not limited to: self-promotion, self-aggrandizement, manipulation, taking advantage of others' weaknesses, practicing fraud, cheating, abusing others' trust, failing to honor our word, being lazy on the job, being greedy, gluttonous, not following health laws and neglecting to take care of our bodies—God's temples, stealing, back-stabbing, disrespecting those in authority, tearing down another's character, wasting time, wasting resources, using people to get what we want, expecting to be waited on hand and foot, always trying to prove we are right, and being defiant when we are corrected.

- *Promises to overcome Ungodly Behaviors:* Romans 12:18-21, 1 Corinthians 10:13.

7. Ungodly Relationships: The most common relationship breaches come from inappropriate relationships between the opposite sexes (both inside and outside of marriage), unbiblical sexual relationships between the same sex, or romantic relationships between a believer and an unbeliever. Emotional adultery and lusts also fit in this category.

- *Promises for victory over Ungodly Relationships:* 2 Corinthians 6:4, and 1 Samuel 16:7.

8. Worldly Preoccupations: Satan's key goal is to get us to love the world rather than God. Breaches include: Status, love of money, love of expensive fashions, expensive cars, excessive love for temporal pleasures. God tells us, "Where our treasure is, there our heart will be also" (Matthew 6:21).

- *Promises for overcoming Worldly Preoccupations:* Colossians 3:1-3, Romans 12:1, 2.

9. Satanic Strongholds: Obviously as Bible believing Christians, there are certain things we should not ever be involved with! Drugs, tobacco, excessive usage of alcohol (or any other addictive substance), including of the occult are off limits for Christians. In addition, a Christian should not have involvement in spiritism, mysticism, psychism, witchcraft, tarot card reading, horoscopes, or the occult. The Bible tells us that there is to be NO fellowship between light and darkness.

- *Promises for overcoming Satanic Strongholds*: 2 Corinthians 10:3-4, and Psalm 40:2, 3.

10. Ungodly sins of Omission: Often we congratulate ourselves on what we are not doing wrong, and fail to recognize what we are not doing right. These "breaches of omission" are the attitudes and lifestyles that God has called us to live as Christians that we often fall so short in such as: truly seeking after God with our whole hearts, true complete heart surrender, abhorrence for our sins and those things that wound Christ afresh, earnestness to receive more of the Holy Spirit which is the only thing that will give us victory over sin, spiritual zeal and life, the fruit of the Spirit in our lives (See Galatians 5:22), faith, humility, trust in God's Word, sincere interest in deep Bible study and prayer, spiritual fortitude and backbone when the battle around us increases against the Truths of God's Word, self-control, warmth and love toward our brethren, friendliness toward strangers and those different from us, kindness and willingness to

sacrifice for the poor and for the least of these, willingness to be inconvenienced to help others in need, taking up our cross daily and denying ourselves for the sake of the gospel, willingness to wrestle and agonize in prayer for others, desire and effort to stand in the gap as intercessors for a perishing land, pain over how we hinder and hold back God's work by our spiritual apathy, and the list goes on and on.

- Promises for Forgiveness of Sins of Omission: 1 John 1:9, Ephesians 2:8-9, Jeremiah 33:3.

Thankfully we are told that Christ came to set the captives free, to make our crooked ways straight, and to break apart the chains that bind us (see Isaiah 58:6).

In your prayer today, make earnest, thorough work for repentance. Take hold of your own case, and by humble confession stand clear before God.

LOG-OFF: DAY 28 – Evening Prayers

Spend some time praying with these prayer points. You can stay on each point for five minutes as needed:

1. Under the covering of the Superior Blood of Jesus Christ, I reject any spirit of pride, stubbornness, ingratitude, and wickedness that finds its way to operate in and through me.
2. Under the covering of the Superior Blood of Jesus Christ, I rebuke any spirit of gossip working in and through me. I reject it.
3. Under the covering of the Superior Blood of Jesus Christ, I refuse to be a co-conspirator and an associate to destroy, harm, tarnish, blackmail, and assassinate the character of a fellow Christian. I refuse to stand in the counsel of ungodliness, and evil practitioners.
4. Under the covering of the Superior Blood of Jesus Christ, I release the Fire of God, the Blood of Jesus and destroy the power of all curses, hexes, vexes, spells, charms, fetishes, blood sacrifices and demonic fasting, operating against my family and my church.
5. Under the covering of the Superior Blood of Jesus Christ, I release the Fire of God, the Blood of Jesus and destroy the power of all psychic: prayers, thoughts, projections, power, and warfare.
6. Under the covering of the Superior Blood of Jesus Christ, I plead the blood against all diabolical portals; all witchcraft, all-natural artifacts of witchcraft, sorcery, magic, voodoo, all manipulation and mind control against my divine hedge and the hedge of the church I attend in Jesus' name.
7. Under the covering of the Superior Blood of Jesus Christ, I release the Fire of God, the Blood of Jesus and destroy the power of all jinxes, potions, bewitchments, death, destruction, sickness, pain, torment, prayer chains, incense and candle burning.

8. Under the covering of the Superior Blood of Jesus Christ, I release the Fire of God, the Blood of Jesus and destroy the power of all demoniacal incantations, chanting, blessings, hoodoo, crystals, root works, eggs and cancel all curses being sent to me, my family, Church and anyone associated with me in any way.
9. Under the covering of the Superior Blood of Jesus Christ, I now seal up their powers within themselves, so that they cannot use them against anyone, and that their works are destroyed, NOW, in the hope that their souls might be saved for the Glory of God.
10. Under the covering of the Superior Blood of Jesus Christ, I release the Love of God to them in the Name and by the Blood of JESUS CHRIST, AMEN.

DAY 29
The Ministry of Restoration

*"And your ancient ruins shall be rebuilt; you shall raise up the foundations of many generations; you shall be called the repairer of the breach, the **restorer of streets to dwell in**." – Isaiah 58:12*

DAY 29 – The Ministry of Restoration

We must continue to examine ourselves during the fasting. You should not complete this fast without doing due diligence for yourself. You cannot afford to end it unaccomplished. Do it the right way now.

LOG-ON: DAY 29 – Morning Prayers

Spend at least five minutes, confess, declare and pray on each prayer point as necessary:

1. Under the covering of the Superior Blood of Jesus Christ, OH LORD, lift up the hedge of your salvation and deliverance around my life, my family and my church in Jesus' name.
2. Under the covering of the Superior Blood of Jesus Christ, Oh LORD, let the hedge of righteousness be lifted around my name in Jesus' name.
3. Under the covering of the Blood of Jesus Christ, I eat the Body of Jesus Christ and drink His Blood (John 6:54).
4. Under the covering of the Blood of Jesus Christ, I have redemption through the Blood of Jesus Christ and I am redeemed from the power of evil (Eph. 1:7).
5. Under the covering of the Blood of Jesus Christ, I rebuke and cast out all spirits of torment and fear because I have peace through the Blood of Jesus Christ (Col. 1:20).
6. Under the covering of the Blood of Jesus Christ, I receive the benefits of the New Covenant through the Blood of Jesus Christ (Matt. 26:28).
7. Under the covering of the Blood of Jesus Christ, I receive healing and health through the Blood of Jesus Christ (1 Pet. 2:24).

8. Under the covering of the Blood of Jesus Christ, let every power contrary to the power of God operating to suppress people in my area be neutralized, in the name of Jesus.
9. Under the covering of the Blood of Jesus Christ, I bind every spirit of frustration, defeat, delayed blessing and fear in my community, in the name of Jesus.
10. Under the covering of the Blood of Jesus Christ, I banish every enemy of progress in my neighborhood, in the name of Jesus.

DAY 29

The Ministry of Restoration

*"And your ancient ruins shall be rebuilt; you shall raise up the foundations of many generations; you shall be called the repairer of the breach, the **restorer of streets to dwell in**." – Isaiah 58:12*

THIS MONTH, I FEEL that the Lord is calling us once again to address the issue of Restoration. Restoration comes in various and diverse dimensions; in the physical as well as the spiritual realm. Men and women always work at restoring things, mostly in the natural or physical dimension. For example, restoring a house to its original state, restoring relationships and things like equipment, tools or artifacts and monuments. In doing so, the approach, in most cases is always with human knowledge and wisdom. In some cases, and for particular cases, this may work. For example, in the case of restoring a house, monuments, artifact and even possessions. This is made possible through the available body of human knowledge and advances in science and technology.

However, the spiritual dimension of restoration is not always so. Issues that have spiritual implications, even if they are physical, many times result in disaster if approached with human knowledge. In this stage of our fasting, I want to address spiritual restoration. This will include issues of our lives, our relationships, work, business, health and leadership in our nation. In many of these cases, there are breaches that need to be repaired for restoration to take place. Jesus is the master repairer of breaches, and He has chosen to share the role of repairer with us. He makes use of human elements as the channel to bring about the restoration. The LORD requires us to be agents for the restoration that He wants to accomplish in the various spiritual dimensions of our existence, as earlier enumerated. For example, He may use a spouse to bring restoration to their marriage or to the marriage of others. He will use willing and ready hands to bring about His purpose in the world.

I am persuaded that the LORD is calling us into the ministry of restoration. He wants to use us to restore issues in our lives and the lives of others. He wants us to be the agents of restoration in our part of the world on His behalf. However, to qualify, we must make ourselves meet the requirements presented here throughout our fasting. The restorer of paths to dwell in must be wholly given to fasting, and must practice the kind of fast that God has chosen. Will you be that restorer for this generation? For your family? For your church? There are marriages and relationships in need of restoration. Our nations need restoration. We must rise up at this time to the work of repairing the breaches and be restorers of streets to dwell in. The Lord bless us as we make ourselves available. May the Lord bless and keep you. May He make His face to shine upon you and be gracious unto you. May the Lord lift up His countenance upon you and give you peace, now and forevermore. Amen.

LOG OFF: DAY 29 – Evening Prayers

Confess and declare these prayer points, and spend at least five minutes on each, as you deem fit:

1. Under the covering of the Superior Blood of Jesus Christ, I confess and declare that You alone are Almighty, and there is no other God besides You. (Spend time to adore the LORD).

2. Under the covering of the Superior Blood of Jesus Christ, I confess and declare, I am a member of the LORD's vanguard and called to be a transformer in my family, and church.

3. Under the covering of the Superior Blood of Jesus Christ, I confess and declare, I am a repairer of breaches and the restorer of streets to dwell in, both in the lives of others and even in my own life and that of my church, and nation.

4. Under the covering of the Superior Blood of Jesus Christ, I pray for restoration in all Christian marriages and relationships. I bless them with fresh wine, peace and joy.

5. Under the covering of the Superior Blood of Jesus Christ, I pray for Christian parents whose relationships with their children have broken down irreparably and for children who have turned against their parents. (If you are in this situation, pray that the Lord will help you to deal with the issues involved, to forget the past and look forward to a future in Christ.

6. Under the covering of the Superior Blood of Jesus Christ, O LORD bring into my life agents of

restoration who will help me to repair the breaches that separate me from you, and hinder my destiny.

7. Under the covering of the Superior Blood of Jesus Christ, I pray for my nation, and ask the Lord to raise agents of restoration in deed and in truth who will help repair the breaches and make our streets to become places of joy, progress, and peace.

8. Under the covering of the Superior Blood of Jesus Christ, I declare, all stubborn problems facing me at the moment will be a thing of the past. I declare I will experience tremendous growth and progress this month.

9. Under the covering of the Superior Blood of Jesus Christ, I pray for our world. My Father, arise and frustrate every counsel of the evil one against the Church legislated in the system of the world's court.

10. Under the covering of the Superior Blood of Jesus Christ, I declare and decree the Kingdom of our God will come and His counsel shall prevail in our world.

DAY 30
The Master Repairer

*"And your ancient ruins shall be rebuilt; you shall raise up the foundations of many generations; **you shall be called the repairer of the breach**, the restorer of streets to dwell in." – Isaiah 58:12*

DAY 30 – The Master Repairer

We have come to the end of this great spiritual journey. It is my prayer, hope, and faith that the LORD has in some special way visited you during this experience. In this last chapter, I want to share with you, how the young carpenter form Nazareth will fix you up and make you whole. He is the Master Repairer of all breaches.

LOG-ON: DAY 30 – Morning Prayers

Spend at least five minutes, confess, declare and pray on each prayer point as necessary:

11. Under the covering of the Blood of Jesus Christ, I bind the spirit of death, cancer and poverty in my city, in the name of Jesus.
12. Under the covering of the Blood of Jesus Christ, I reject, renounce and destroy every evil agreement or covenant in my city, in the name of Jesus.
13. Under the covering of the Blood of Jesus Christ, I nullify the effects and operation of evil forces around my neighborhood, in the name of Jesus.
14. Under the covering of the Blood of Jesus Christ, Lord, get all my stubborn pursuers occupied with unprofitable assignments, in the name of Jesus.
15. Under the covering of the Blood of Jesus Christ, I fire back every arrow, spiritual bullets and satanic missiles fired at my church.
16. Under the covering of the Blood of Jesus Christ, Father Lord, make me a repairer of the breach, a restorer of paths to dwell in, a builder of lives, and contractor of foundations, in Jesus' name.
17. Under the covering of the Blood of Jesus Christ,

Father, let the source of my financial income never go dry in Jesus' name.

18. Under the covering of the Blood of Jesus Christ, Father, bless my basket and bless my waters.

19. Under the covering of the Blood of Jesus Christ, Father, as I go out looking for my daily bread, I will not become a prey to the enemy in Jesus' name.

20. Under the covering of the Blood of Jesus Christ, any principality who continues to oppress people in this community, may the earth open and swallow you up in Jesus' name.

DAY 30

The Master Repairer

*"And your ancient ruins shall be rebuilt; you shall raise up the foundations of many generations; **you shall be called the repairer of the breach**, the restorer of streets to dwell in." – Isaiah 58:12*

WE HAVE AN IMPORTANT WORK TO DO. The second law of thermodynamics is that unless there is an input of information and or energy, all material things will deteriorate, decay and eventually fall apart. That is why paper bags disintegrate, and food perishes, and cars need maintenance, and houses need to be repaired.

Solomon's Temple was one of the greatest edifices of the ancient world. It was the permanent structure that was envisioned by King David and built by Solomon his son.

Through this temple, God would teach His people and the world the way of salvation. The temple was to be the center of religious activity for God's people, the center for mission, and where the presence of God would abide.

Given the reality of the second law of thermodynamics it was bound to experience some wear and tear. Two stories are given in the Bible telling us when major repair work was done on the "breaches" of the temple.

Temple repairs were needed by 835 B.C., and at this time it was initiated and completed under King Joash. By around 620 B.C. the temple again needed repairs and this was done under the leadership of King Josiah. By 586 B.C the temple was destroyed by the armies of Nebuchadnezzar. In 515 B.C., under the leadership of Zerubbabel, the temple was rebuilt when the exiles returned home from Babylon.

Here were the people of God taking care of the house of God. It wasn't beneath them, they recognized the importance of the work, and they gave themselves to repairing the breach.

Like this temple of old, churches today need to be taken care of. God expects our best when it comes to His house. Today God is looking for repairers of the breach – but in more than one way:

> *"Those from among you shall build the old waste places; you shall raise up the foundations of many generations; and you shall be called the repairer of the breach, the restorer of streets to dwell in." (Isa. 58:12)*

In the immediate context of this verse, the prophet was letting God's people know that after time spent in Babylon and when they returned home, the temple, the city, the walls would need to be rebuilt. Talk about a breach! And those who would go back and work to rebuild their city would be called "repairers of the breach." But this verse isn't just referring to a people repairing physical buildings. This verse has tremendous spiritual connotations.

At that time, God did not just want His people to repair houses, fences, and walls. The city's moral edifice was in ruins, and needed to be rebuilt also. This call for spiritual renewal, reformation and restoration was not just to be made for Zerubbabel's era, but for all time.

The repairing of the breaches in the ancient temple at the hands of King Joash, King Josiah, and Zerubbabel serve as an illustration of the work God has given His people to do throughout time until today. Each brick laid represented one more piece of Biblical truth discovered. Each application of mortar represented God calling His children out of the world and darkness into genuine faith. Each breach repaired represented someone accepting Jesus Christ as Lord and Savior and standing firm on the truths of the eternal Word of God.

There is no question today that you and I are called to be repairers of the breach. But the master Repairer of the Breach is Jesus. In Joash, in Josiah, and in Zerubbabel, we witness the work of Jesus. That means whatever is broken in your life, Jesus, the Master Builder and Architect, can restore it.

We live in a broken world and we have all been affected. We have all been touched by brokenness. If a relationship is broken, Jesus is the Repairer of the Breach. If your marriage is on the rocks, Jesus is the Repairer of the Breach. If your children seem out of control and they have no respect for you, Jesus is the Repairer of the Breach. If you have been hurt by someone's words or actions, if you are wounded and you are broken, Jesus is the Repairer of the Breach.

Today, in Christ's stead, I appeal to you and point you to the One who can and will make wrongs right, who can take what is broken and fix it. He can take that breach in your life and restore you into His image. It's for His glory you know. It's something He's good at. If you would come to Him in your need and in your brokenness, He will make you whole.

LOG OFF: DAY 30 – Evening Prayers

Confess and declare these prayer points, and spend at least five minutes on each, as you deem fit:

1. Under the covering of the Blood of Jesus Christ, LORD, I declare according to your Word, give us this community, and city for our inheritance. Remove the shackles of demonic oppression and let your Spirit engage in soul winning with us in Jesus' name.
2. Under the covering of the Blood of Jesus Christ, I nullify every negative report ever made about me.
3. Under the covering of the Blood of Jesus Christ, I cease to be a picture of failure. I cease to be abased, rejected, forsaken, desolate and downcast.
4. Under the covering of the Blood of Jesus Christ, I begin to operate as the head and not the tail. I begin to be a true worshiper of Jehovah El-Shaddai and I begin from now to continually praise Him and confess positively.
5. Under the covering of the Blood of Jesus Christ, I decree a realignment of the situation around Christians, to favor them in this country, in the name of Jesus.
6. Under the covering of the Blood of Jesus Christ, I dethrone every strange king, installed in the spirit over this country, in the name of Jesus.
7. Under the covering of the Blood of Jesus Christ, let all principalities, powers, rulers of darkness and spiritual wickedness in heavenly places, militating against this nation be bound and disgraced, in the name of Jesus.

8. Under the covering of the Blood of Jesus Christ, let righteousness reign, in every part of this nation, in Jesus' name.

9. Under the covering of the Superior Blood of Jesus Christ, I begin to operate at the head and not the tail. I begin to be a true worshiper of Jehovah El-Shaddai and I begin from now to continually praise Him and confess positively.

10. Under the covering of the Superior Blood of Jesus Christ, O Lord, let me experience the force, energy and impulses of Thy Spirit.

Postface
Breaking the Fast

The most difficult period is immediately after the fast. This period requires more discipline and self-control than any other time of the fast. Reintroduce food very gradually. Suggestions for breaking the fast:

- Day 1: Break on fruits every 2 hours.

- Day 2 to 3: Over the next 3 days, gradually increase the amount of food and the interval between feedings. Fresh fruits, lettuce, steamed vegetables, baked sweet potato or other light meals are recommended.

- Day 4: By now, 3 normal-sized meals can be tolerated.

A Word of Caution

1. The stomach is very sensitive after the fast so be careful not to eat fruit that is too ripe as this may cause stomach cramping and pain.

2. Overeating too early after the fast may result in pain and vomiting.

3. Spicy food, too much salt and pepper taken soon after the fasting could irritate and cause damage to the stomach lining.

4. Always remember to start with a little of everything new and build up gradually. Avoid cakes, pastries and biscuits. Remember these golden rules:
- Watch your quantities.
- Eat slowly and masticate well.
- Stop at the first warning sign.
- Rest as much as possible.
- Don't try to do to much too soon.

5. If any difficulty arises it is because you are rushing the breaking-in period. The remedy is to eat less, or cut out some of the food. If necessary, go back to fruit juices or fresh fruit again. Do not rush your stomach, the more slowly you get back to regular eating, the better will be your physical condition afterward. Do not be discouraged if at any time during the fast you fell into temptation and ate. Pick yourself up and try again. Satan will not give up tempting you but the Lord is our strength.

Testimony

In the last 30 days has God given you a fasting testimony?

Has God given you a fasting testimony regarding: experiencing the sweetness of His presence? Enjoying the wonders of His grace? Discovering His guiding hand in a major decision? Finding a new sense of freedom and healing from the hurts of the past? Realizing a victory over a nagging area of sin in your life? Embracing a spiritual breakthrough in your ministry?

How has God shown up in your life in the last 30 days of fasting? If He has, write it down, share it with a friend and reflect upon it with a thankful heart.

If He hasn't, keep fasting until He does. Be determined like Jacob who wrestled with God and would not let Him go until He blessed him. In this, Jacob experienced the transformational power of God that marked not only his life in that moment but also his descendants for eternity.

May we experience what Jesus taught his disciples, "Blessed are those who hunger and thirst for righteousness, for they will be filled". (Matthew 5:6).

www.ingramcontent.com/pod-product-compliance
Lightning Source LLC
Chambersburg PA
CBHW062005180426
43198CB00037B/2428